JOHN AND DONALD BAILLIE

SELECTED WRITINGS

Edited by
David A S Fergusson

THE DEVOTIONAL LIBRARY

GENERAL EDITORS: PROFESSOR JAMES B TORRANCE
AND DR MICHAEL JINKINS

SAINT ANDREW PRESS
EDINBURGH

First published in 1997 by
SAINT ANDREW PRESS
121 George Street, Edinburgh EH2 4YN

Copyright Part I: *Introduction* (pp 1-12) © David A S Fergusson 1997

Copyright Part II: *Selected Writings* (pp 13-153) © Ian F Baillie 1997

The extracts from the work of John and Donald Baillie selected for this volume have been used with the permission of Ian Baillie. The publisher and editor would like to express their gratitude for permission granted.

ISBN 0 7152 0718 0

British Library Cataloguing in Publication Data
A catalogue record for this book
is available from the British Library.

ISBN 0715207180

The Publisher acknowledges financial assistance from The Drummond Trust towards the publication of this volume.

Cover and **design concept** by Mark Blackadder.
Typeset in Garamond.
Printed and **bound** by BPC-AUP Aberdeen Ltd.

CONTENTS

JOHN AND DONALD BAILLIE
Part I: *An Introduction*

JOHN AND DONALD BAILLIE
Part II: *Selected Writings*

CONTENTS

General Editors' Foreword

THE editors of 'The Devotional Library' are pleased to present the second sequence of books in this important series designed to provide ministers, lay persons and students of theology with the finest devotional thought from great theologians. Previously the series has featured the devotional reflections of *John Knox* (by Henry Sefton), *Thomas Erskine* (Trevor Hart) and *John McLeod Campbell* (Michael Jinkins). This new sequence features *John and Donald Baillie* (David Fergusson), *Edward Irving* (Graham McFarlane) and *George MacDonald* (Gary and Cathy Deddo).

In a time when shops are crowded with books on spirituality and mysticism that sometimes fail to live up to their advertisements, we think it is valuable to return to deeper and richer well-springs of Christian devotional thought, to thinkers renowned for loving God with their minds. The authors of these volumes are themselves scholars intimately familiar with these Christian thinkers and appreciative of the spiritual life of the Christian. They provide in each book a lively and informative introduction to the life and thought of the theologian and an anthology of that person's devotional writings.

As one reads these classical selections, one may well come to a new and more radical understanding of what it means to be a 'theologian' – that is, a person who lives in and under the Word (*logos*) of God (*theos*). Indeed, these theologians encourage us all to discover our own 'theological' vocation, the call of Christ which comes to each of us to hear and receive with joy the Word who gives us life. Our prayer is that 'The Devotional Library' will provide its readers with a vast resource of devotional literature in the English language, so that we may learn what it means to live as Christians from people whose own lives have been shaped by prayer, reflection and response to this Word.

GENERAL EDITORS
Reverend Professor James B Torrance
Reverend Dr Michael Jinkins

Author's
Preface

Both John and Donald Baillie were university theologians and ministers of the church. In preparing this volume I have been struck once more by the intellectual keenness and spiritual intensity of their writings, and I remain convinced that this fusion of qualities needs to be recaptured on both sides.

I am grateful to the series editors for their invitation to compile this collection, to Lesley Taylor at Saint Andrew Press for her advice in the editorial process, and to Teresa Clark and Morton Gauld of the Department of Divinity with Religious Studies here at Aberdeen University for their assistance with the photocopying of materials.

Editor
David Fergusson
King's College, Old Aberdeen

JOHN AND DONALD BAILLIE

Part I: *An Introduction*

BIOGRAPHY[1]

TWO brothers, John Baillie (1886-1960) and Donald Baillie (1887-1954), were arguably the most distinguished Scottish theologians of the mid twentieth century. They were the elder of three sons born to Revd John Baillie, a Free Church minister in Gairloch in the West Highlands of Scotland, and his wife Annie MacPherson. Their third son, Peter, was tragically killed in a drowning accident in India in 1914.

The Baillies lost their father in early childhood, and in 1891 were taken by their mother to live in Inverness. After schooling at Inverness Royal Academy they moved to Edinburgh where the three boys underwent a university education. Both John and Donald took first class honours degrees in philosophy before training for the ministry at New College, which was at that time one of three seminaries in the United Free Church. Like many budding Scottish theological scholars they took advantage of the opportunity to study in Germany, and at different times both sat under Wilhelm Herrmann in Marburg. After serving as assistant ministers in Edinburgh, they worked for the Young Men's Christian Association (YMCA) in France during the time of the Great War.

Donald's time of service in France was brief due to the indifferent health and frequent bouts of asthma which afflicted him for most of his life. He returned to Scotland to pastoral ministry and served in a succession of United Free Church (and after the union of 1929, Church of Scotland) charges in St Boswells, Inverbervie, Cupar, and finally Kilmacolm. In 1934 he was appointed to the new Chair of Systematic Theology at St Mary's College in the University of St Andrews, a post which he held until his death in 1954. During this time he gained an international reputation as the author of *God was in Christ* (1948) and attracted students from across the world to St Andrews. He was a lifelong bachelor.

After the war, John held several academic posts in North America – at Auburn Seminary, New York (1919-27); Emmanuel College, Toronto (1927-30); and Union Seminary, New York (1930-34) – before returning to the Chair of Divinity in the University of Edinburgh in 1934. He was the author of numerous books, mainly in philosophical and apologetic theology, and he also exercised a powerful influence on the life of the national and international Church. He was appointed Moderator of the General Assembly in 1943, and was one of six Presidents of the World Council of Churches at Evanston in 1954. In 1956 he retired from his chair, having served also as Dean of the Faculty of Divinity and Principal of New College. He died in 1960 shortly before he was due to deliver the Gifford Lectures in Edinburgh. John was married to Florence Jewel in 1919. They had one son, Ian, who now lives in retirement in Edinburgh.

The Baillies' work shows a remarkable theological harmony, and, despite the differences in their personalities (or perhaps because of them), they remained in the closest personal and intellectual friendship throughout their lives. If John was the more robust and imperious of the two, whose career scaled greater heights, then Donald displayed a sensitivity and warmth which enabled him to be a much loved pastor to his congregations and students. After Donald's death it is said that John never regained his former zest, and he once confessed that never a day passed when he did not miss Donald's company.[2]

THEOLOGY

In their theological work the Baillies reflected the tension that they had experienced since their school days between the Calvinist heritage of their Free Church manse and the humanist culture of their education. They were taught from their earliest years the Shorter Catechism, but became acutely conscious both of its failure to appreciate the world of art and literature, and also of the need to respond to the complex theological challenges posed by the philosophy and biblical scholarship of the previous 150 years. In the face of this collision of Calvinist Christianity with the world of the Renaissance and the Enlightenment, the Baillies succeeded in producing in their theological writings (which reveal almost total unanimity) a blend of Christian orthodoxy and openness to the world of philosophy, literature and social theory. This can be illustrated in several ways.

(a) In what might be called their fundamental theology, both John and Donald Baillie argued that the source of our awareness of God is found in our experience of value. Whatever difficulties the traditional arguments for the existence of God may encounter one cannot doubt the primary deliverances of the moral conscience which inform us inescapably of what our duties are. That we are obliged to act in conformity with moral laws is a fact that can only be elucidated transcendentally. The seriousness of moral claims demands a theological explanation; only God can be the source of our inescapable sense of moral obligation. We find both Baillies pursuing this line of argument in their first books. Returning from the war, John argued that the soldier's abiding sense of duty and comradeship contained the germ of a religious faith[3], while Donald in his Kerr lectures confronted those who were perplexed by religious doubt with the thought that our being morally obliged leads, if we will but follow the clue, to an awareness of God.[4] The Baillies never appeared to abandon this approach, although there are some signs that they were conscious that this description of the moral consciousness looked less appropriate in an age when moral value and religious belief were becoming increasingly dissociated.

(b) On the subject of our knowledge of God, their most original contribution comes in John's concept of 'mediated immediacy'.[5] By the use of this apparent contradiction he seeks to show that our knowledge of God is both mediate and yet direct. It comes to us in, with and under other forms of awareness – the natural world, other people, the Bible and the humanity of Christ – yet in these we are aware of God and do not know him merely by inference or by argument. In order to demonstrate the plausibility of this notion of 'mediated immediacy', John argues persuasively that the very same phenomenon occurs in our knowledge of other people. The concept of 'mediated immediacy' remains worthy of serious theological attention.

(c) In their handling of the central themes in Christian doctrine the Baillies generally attempted to do justice to the formulations of orthodoxy, but in such a way as to reckon with the problems of modernity. Both show an openness to the results of biblical scholarship, to trends within twentieth century theology – their books are replete with references to Barth, Bultmann, Brunner, Tillich and Niebuhr – and to the insights of Christian traditions outwith their own Calvinist heritage. According to the Baillies, there is a unique and redemptive knowledge of God in Jesus Christ, but this does not exclude the possibility of a knowledge of God in other religions and traditions outwith the Christian. This was a source of sharp disagreement between John Baillie and his Swiss contemporary, Karl Barth.[6]

The most significant work the Baillies produced in the area of Christian doctrine was unquestionably Donald's *God was in Christ* (1948). In the forty years since its publication this has become something of a modern classic and is discussed in several recent christological studies.[7] Here we find Donald trying to make sense of the traditional doctrines of the incarnation, the atonement and the Trinity in the light of our shared Christian experience. In particular, he appeals to what he calls 'the paradox of grace'. It is the experience of every Christian man and woman that each good deed performed is never more free and human than when we can attribute the work not to ourselves but wholly to the grace of God within us. 'I ... though not I but the grace of God which is with me' (I Corinthians 15:10). We see this paradox of grace throughout the human existence of Jesus. In him it is complete and all-controlling. When we understand this as the constitution of his earthly existence we can make sense of the claim that he is both fully human and yet fully divine. There is nothing within the life of Jesus of which we cannot say that it reveals both himself and yet is wholly the work of God. This treatment of the paradox of grace has fascinated commentators. If its weakness is that it fails to make sense of the uniqueness of Jesus as the Son of God become human, we should be aware that Donald Baillie insisted that it was at most an analogy and that our own experience of grace was dependent upon that unique and perfect embodiment of grace we find in Christ.[8]

(d) The Baillies' theology is also characterised by an apologetic style. They spoke consciously for those beset by doubt, those who struggled to accept some aspect of Christian teaching, and those who struggled to persevere in the Christian life. As apologists for the Christian faith their measure of success in reaching a wide audience was probably due to the lucidity and elegance of their style, their own personal struggles, their involvement in the life of the Church, and their sensitivity to those they encountered throughout their lives. Their most influential apologetic work was perhaps John's *Invitation to Pilgrimage* (1942), based on a series of lectures delivered at the beginning of the Second World War. Earlier he had written in the aftermath of the First World War: 'When I turned again to my old pursuits after the war was over, the khaki figures still seemed to keep their place in the background of my mind, and in much of what I have written since these days a clairvoyant reader may find them haunting the margins of the page.'[9]

CHURCH AND SOCIETY[10]

The Baillies' lives were marked by a commitment both to academic theology and to the wider work of the Church. Murdo Ewen Macdonald has commented on the way in which theology, teaching, preaching and pastoral ministry formed an 'organic unity' in their work.[11] Throughout their writings we find them returning again and again to the significance of the Church as the community in which God is known through Jesus Christ in the fellowship of the Holy Spirit. Even in their more philosophical treatises there is an unembarrassed recollection of their debt to the Highland Calvinism in which they were brought up. Their appropriation of this tradition may at times have been critical, yet it is frequently acknowledged as a positive influence upon their personal and intellectual pilgrimage. A good example of this is the extraordinary opening to *And the Life Everlasting*:

Among the very earliest pictures my memory provides is one which though I see it but dimly, has come back to me again and again during the preparation of the following pages. I am sitting on my father's knee in the day-nursery of a manse in the Scottish Highlands, contentedly gazing into the fire which burns brightly on the hearth. My father asks me which is the chief end of man and I reply, with perfect readiness, that man's chief end is to glorify God and to enjoy Him forever. This is, of course, the first question and answer of the Shorter Catechism .... My own infant capacity must have been very weak indeed, for 'chief-end' was to me a single word, and a word whose precise meaning was beyond my imagining. But I did grasp, I think, even then, something of the general teaching that was meant to be conveyed, and I grew up understanding and believing that only in the everlasting enjoyment of God's presence could my life ever reach its proper and divinely appointed fulness.

John Baillie's commitment to the affairs of the Church in which he was raised was renewed upon his return to Edinburgh in 1934. In the ensuing years he became a distinguished preacher and church leader within Scotland and in 1940 was invited to convene the important 'Commission for the Interpretation of God's Will in the Present Crisis'. This commission produced a series of reports during the war years which prepared the Church for the ecclesiastical, social and global changes that were to take place after 1945. Baillie presented these reports to the Assembly from 1941-45 and established a reputation as an effective and forward-looking convener. The commission boldly tackled a range of issues including the ethics of artificial contraception, the evils of colonialism, the need for a greater measure of public control over the means of production, and the desirability of reforms within the church including the ordination of women elders. The findings of the commission commanded the support of a majority within the General Assembly – it also resonated with many of the themes of the Beveridge Report – and although not all its recommendations were implemented forthwith, its significance for the post-war Church of Scotland is now widely recognised.[12] In particular, its claim that the Church has a duty to speak critically to the civic order was vehemently defended, and foreshadowed many of the stances adopted by the General Assembly's Church and Nation Committee in the post-war period.

In 1943 John Baillie was elected Moderator of the General Assembly. The son of a Free Church Minister, he served at the time of the centenary of the Disruption. From his closing address to the General Assembly we catch a glimpse of the theological and social issues which preoccupied him during the war years. The decline in the social significance of the Church – a process often described as secularization – troubled him and he laboured with the twin thoughts that the Church had both to re-establish its hold over the hearts and minds of the population, and that there remained much goodness, beauty and truth outwith its walls. His awareness of this problem was in part conditioned by his involvement with the Moot, a small association of Christian intellectuals including T S Eliot, J H Oldham and Karl Mannheim, which met regularly as a 'brainstorming' group throughout the 1930s and 40s. John Baillie's preoccupation with the theological problems concerning the relationship of church to society can be seen in three volumes from this period: *Invitation to Pilgrimage* (1942); *What is Christian Civilization?* (1945); and *The Belief in Progress* (1950).

The Baillies were also highly committed ecumenists. This was evident not only in their teaching and writings which drew upon the richness and diversity of the theological traditions of the Church, but also in their involvement with ecumenical bodies. Both participated in the work of the World Council of Churches and its parent bodies: Donald as a prominent member of the Faith and Order Commission and John as a member of the Central Committee of the WCC before becoming one of six Presidents at the WCC General Assembly in Evanston, 1954. Lesslie Newbigin has penned some interesting reflections on Baillie's role at the WCC amongst the world's leading theologians.

Baillie was a member of the famous committee of 25 theologians, which included Barth, Brunner, Niebuhr, Vogel, Wingren, Schlink and others on the theme of the Evanston Assembly – 'Christ, the Hope of the World' – generally known as the 25 hopeless theologians. Unlike Niebuhr, who was so incensed by Barth that he threatened to walk out, Baillie always kept his cool but made his points.

Donald was also a distinguished member of Faith and Order until his death and took part in the Lund Conference in 1952. He co-edited the volume on Intercommunion, and became Convener of the Church of Scotland Committee on Inter-Church Relations and for several years served as the chairman of the sub-commission on Intercommunion. In his writings on the sacraments and in his insistence upon the value of celebrating all the seasons of the Christian year, one finds an ecumenical openness to the intellectual and spiritual riches of other traditions. The following personal testimony to Donald bears witness to this:

You often have the adjective 'staunch' applied to a Presbyterian; it is less often that 'devout' is applied. Yet that is the kind of Presbyterian that Dr Baillie was, and it was that which attracted me most of all to him. Perhaps it is that trait which made him so greatly esteemed by people ranging from Baptists to advanced Anglo-Catholics. That devotion was also, I think, the clue to his approach to theology. Whereas the usual way to lecture about the Atonement, for example, is to give most of the time available to a history of the doctrine and to a discussion of the various types of Atonement theory, Dr Baillie covered all that in a few lucid lectures and then spent most of the available time upon what the Atonement really means for us and how we are to conceive it and speak of it to men today. It was that approach to his work – and to people – that made him what some traditions would call an admirable 'Spiritual Director'.[13]

SPIRITUALITY

The spirituality of the Baillies is revealed most clearly in their published collections of sermons and in John's *A Diary of Private*

Prayer (1936) which has been translated into several languages and recently reissued by Oxford University Press. The extracts that have been compiled for this volume are eloquent testimony to their spirituality, but mention might be made also of the following distinctive characteristics:

(a) The Baillies' use of language reflects something of the simplicity and profundity of their Celtic inheritance. They have a capacity to communicate difficult theological ideas in the most lucid terms without ever appearing simplistic or patronising towards their audience. At the same time, they can penetrate to human and religious depths without ever laying siege to the emotions or indulging in verbal haranguing.

(b) The use of illustration in the Baillies' sermons is almost an art form in which a passage of Scripture can be interpreted with arresting effect. Their use of story and incident reveals judicious selection, an economy of words, and an ability to press a range of materials from philosophy, novels, folklore and everyday life into the service of the Word of God.

(c) Their prayers reflect something of the richness of the church's spiritual tradition, perhaps especially the Book of Common Prayer, and they show an ability to express elegantly though simply the ordinary concerns of men and women. It is surely this combination which is the secret of the success of *A Diary of Private Prayer* and explains the succour it has supplied to its thousands of readers.

(d) In their spirituality the Baillies reflect a powerful sense of life as a pilgrimage. As once-born Christians they had an over-riding awareness of the range, variety and opportunities of the Christian life. Their preaching is frequently directed to those who are at difficult stages of life's journey, but always one is left with a sense of the beauty and richness of the Christian faith.

This volume has sought to gather together from the breadth of their output some of their most important devotional writings. At the same time, it includes some of the key sections from their leading theological works and personal reminiscences in order to demonstrate the harmony of mind and heart in John and Donald Baillie.

NOTES TO TEXT

1   I am particularly indebted in this section to Professor Alec Cheyne's 'The Baillie Brothers: A Biographical Introduction' in *Christ, Church and Society: Essays on John Baillie and Donald Baillie* (T&T Clark: Edinburgh, 1993), edited by David Fergusson, pp 3-37.

2   One senses something of the closeness of their relationship in John's biographical introduction to the posthumously published *The Theology of the Sacraments and Other Essays* (Faber & Faber: London, 1957).

3   *The Roots of Religion in the Human Soul* (Hodder & Stoughton: London, 1926). This line of argument is developed in the more technical and scholarly work, *The Interpretation of Religion* (T&T Clark: Edinburgh, 1929).

4   *Faith in God and its Christian Consummation* (T&T Clark: Edinburgh, 1927).

5   *Our Knowledge of God* (Oxford University Press: London, 1939).

6   It is possible, I think, to discern a more sympathetic attitude to the work of Karl Barth in Donald Baillie's writings and unpublished lectures.

7   For example, Schubert Ogden, *The Point of Christology* (SCM: London, 1982), pp 80f; John Macquarrie, *Jesus Christ in Modern Thought* (SCM: London, 1990), pp 327ff.

8   This issue is explored in some depth by John McIntyre in 'The Christology of Donald Baillie in Perspective' in *Christ, Church and Society*, op cit, pp 87-113.

9   'Confessions of a Transplanted Scot' in *Contemporary American Theology: Theological Autobiographies* (Round Table Press: New York, 1933), p 56.

10   I am indebted in this section to Professor Cheyne's 'The Baillies' Churchmanship' in *Christ, Church and Society*, op cit, pp 173-198.

11   *Christ, Church and Society*, op cit, p 282.

12   For a discussion of the work of the Baillie Commission see A R Morton (ed), *God's Will in a Time of Crisis* (Centre for Theology & Public Issues: Edinburgh, 1994).

13 Cited by John Dow in his biographical introduction to *To Whom Shall We Go?*, p 13.

BIBLIOGRAPHY

BOOKS BY JOHN BAILLIE

The Roots of Religion in the Human Soul (Hodder and Stoughton: London, 1926).

The Interpretation of Religion (T&T Clark: Edinburgh, 1929).

The Place of Jesus Christ in Modern Christianity (T&T Clark: Edinburgh, 1929).

And the Life Everlasting (Scribners: New York, 1934; and Oxford University Press: Oxford).

A Diary of Private Prayer (OUP: London, 1936).

Our Knowledge of God (Oxford University Press: London, 1939).

Invitation to Pilgrimage (Oxford University Press: London, 1942).

What is Christian Civilization? (OUP: London, 1945).

The Belief in Progress (Oxford University Press: London, 1950).

The Idea of Revelation in Recent Thought (Oxford University Press: London, 1956).

The Sense of the Presence of God (Oxford University Press: London, 1962).

Christian Devotion (Oxford University Press: London, 1962).

A Reasoned Faith (Oxford University Press: London, 1963).

Baptism and Conversion (Oxford University Press: London, 1964).

BOOKS BY DONALD BAILLIE

Faith in God and its Christian Consummation (T&T Clark: Edinburgh, 1927).

God was in Christ (Faber & Faber: London, 1948).

To Whom Shall We Go? (Saint Andrew Press: Edinburgh, 1955).

The Theology of the Sacraments and Other Essays (Faber & Faber: London, 1957).

Out of Nazareth (Saint Andrew Press: Edinburgh, 1958).

FOR FURTHER DISCUSSION OF THE BAILLIES

D W D Shaw (ed), *In Divers Manners* (St Mary's College: St Andrews, 1990).

David Fergusson (ed), *Christ, Church and Society: Essays on John Baillie and Donald Baillie* (T&T Clark: Edinburgh, 1993).

Andrew Morton (ed), *God's Will in a Time of Crisis* (Centre for Theology and Public Issues: Edinburgh, 1994).

ACKNOWLEDGMENTS

The publisher would like to thank the following sources for the use of material contained within this book:

Pages 108-114: 'University Sermon' taken from the *Cambridge Review* (Cambridge, December 1944, pp 134-135).

Pages 137-138: 'Morning Prayers – Twenty-eighth and Thirtieth Day'; and pages 151-153: 'Evening Prayers – Twenty-sixth and Twenty-first Day' taken from John Baillie: *A Diary of Private Prayer* (Oxford University Press, 1936), by permission of Oxford University Press.

COVER PHOTOGRAPHS

DONALD BAILLIE – from *To Whom Shall We Go?* (Saint Andrew Press: Edinburgh, 1955), photograph © Blackstone Studios, New York.

JOHN BAILLIE – from the *University of Edinburgh Journal* (Edinburgh, Spring 1961).

JOHN AND DONALD BAILLIE
Part II: *Selected Writings*

(A) *Biographical*

1 WEST HIGHLAND UPBRINGING
by John Baillie

THE home into which Donald Baillie was born in November 1887 was a Highland manse presided over by a Calvinist divine of strong character and courtly bearing, and a lady of great charm and goodness; but it was saddened by the father's too early death when Donald, the second of three small boys, was only three years old. A year later our mother moved from Gairloch to Inverness, and it was with home and school life in the Highland capital that our earliest significant memories were associated. Our father's Calvinism had been of the most rigorous and uncompromising kind and, true to the memory of a husband with whom she had lived for only six years, our mother was most anxious that her children's upbringing should be in the same tradition. Her own temperament, if left to itself, might have guided her a little differently, and time brought with it a gradual mellowing of principle, especially after the later move to Edinburgh and its University; until finally she felt herself completely at home under Donald's ministry in his various parishes, sharing all his interests and friendships and delighting in them. Nevertheless it was a very rigid Calvinistic outlook with which we were indoctrinated in our boyhood's home. The system of beliefs embodied in the Westminster standards is of a most remarkable logical self-consistency, once its premises have been allowed, and our mother was not only thoroughly conversant with its intricacies, but well able to answer any objections that might be brought against them. If her sons later developed any aptitudes of a philosophic kind, it was undoubtedly by this home training in theological dialectic that their minds were first sharpened.

The sharpening, however, would have been much less, had it not been for our growing doubts about the trustworthiness of some of the premises on which the system rested. These, as I can now see, were first generated in our minds by the considerably different climate of thought to which we were introduced by what we learned at school. None of us was indeed particularly diligent at his set tasks: Donald used to say in after life that he did no work at school. Nevertheless our minds were awakened and our imaginations stirred by what we heard there, and we were given the keys of what to us, brought up as we had been, was something of a new intellectual kingdom – even if our own independent reading and our eager discussions with some of our fellow scholars had as much to do with the actual unlocking of the doors as what our masters (several of whom were very remarkable men) had to tell us. We were indeed fortunate in our schoolmates. I can think of perhaps eight or ten (spread, however, over several forms) who were of the keenest intellectual quality, and the majority of whom have since rendered conspicuous service in Church and University. Donald's own most particular friend was Jack, now Professor J. Y. Campbell of Westminster College, Cambridge, who went up to the University with him and remained his close friend through all his later life. Together we explored the riches of European literature. Together also we served our own apprenticeship in the literary art, especially in the making of what we thought was poetry.

I have often reflected that parents who dutifully bring up their children in a traditional orthodoxy which has never submitted itself to the challenge of Renaissance and *Aufklärung*, and who then sent them to a school whose whole ethos is of humanist inspiration, seldom realize the extent of the spiritual stress and strain to which they are thus subjecting them. Our minds, for example, were soon set afire by the reading of Shakespeare, but there was no room at all for Shakespeare within the Puritanism of our early upbringing; no room for theatre of any kind; but especially no room for Shakespeare's large and generous and delicately discriminating appreciation of the human scene. Again, we were trained at school to develop a fastidious sense for the weighing of historical evidence, and for distinguishing fact from legend; but our training at home did not allow us to practise this skill on the Bible stories. Or once more, we were abruptly introduced to the world-view of modern science, and we could not make it square with the up-and-down, three-storey geocentric universe of the Biblical writers and of our Catechisms, or with their assumptions about the natural history of the human race.

Donald especially was from an early age haunted with religious doubts of this general kind. Having a very sensitive conscience in the matter, he was fearful of unsettling the minds of others by any mention of them, so that it was not until our undergraduate days that I myself was aware of their existence, but I remember how he then said to me, 'If I had only known that your mind had been troubled in the same way, how great would have been the relief of sharing!' For the strain on his spirit was indeed acute. His only confidante was his mother. This may seem surprising in view of what I have already said, but actually it was not so, for the two had from the first been bound together by the closest possible ties of affection and mutual respect. Yet it says much for our mother that she was able to enter so sympathetically and so understandingly into a trouble so remote from anything she herself had ever suffered.

With it all Donald was full of the joy of life, eager to be out of doors as soon as released from school and, in those bicycling days, fond of exploring with a brother or a friend the near-by country-side. Shy and diffident by nature, especially in his approach to strangers, he was none the less full of fun and banter, and had a prettier wit than any of us. His brothers often chaffed him in after life about the remark, couched in the discreet obscurity of the Gaelic language but well enough understood by us, of an old lady who was struck by his failure to enter into the small talk of the hour in my mother's drawing-room: '*Chan 'eil guth aig Dòmhnull.*' But the boy thus accused of 'having no voice' was both then and afterwards the life of many a congenial company.

Though so fortunate in our school-fellows, we brothers were probably always one another's greatest friends. In our earliest years we had been thrown all the more closely together by the scrupulous care our mother exercised in the selection of our permitted play-mates, though I hasten to add that it was the manners and morals of their homes rather than the social standing of these that controlled her choice. Thus as boys we developed a sort of small-scale 'primitive culture' of our own. We had our own code of *mores,* our own taboos. We invented most of our own games and some of our own romances. We coined innumerable words to denote phenomena and connote shades of meaning for which we did not know the accepted ones. We had our own private names for many lanes and by-ways discovered in our rambles which perhaps nobody had thought it necessary to name before – but they had a significance for some of our games. We had our own names for certain shades of colour, such as 'moon-colour', and Donald and I might on occasion, when we were together, use them until the end of his life. We were interested in identifying the wild flowers, including the weeds in our garden; but we had nobody to tell us their recog-nized names, nor did we even guess that anybody had ever taken the trouble to name them; so we invented names of our own, many of which I still remember. But there were indeed many regions in which we were similarly forced back on our own resources. We had clearly identified in ourselves and others the innocent presence of a phenomenon which in its psychopathic extremes was after-wards to receive the name of compulsion-neurosis, but our private name for it was 'dooarts', that is, things that one felt one had to do, though without sense of reason, such as touching every second lamp-post as one walked down the street.

When our father died, our mother resolved that all three of her sons should follow in his footsteps as ministers of the Church, though this plan was afterwards so far varied as to encourage the youngest to be a missionary doctor. I cannot remember a time when we did not already know that this was what lay in store for us, nor was there ever a time when we did not, to say the least, accept it without demur. But our mother's resolve was really an astonishing one, since our father, who had never enjoyed more than the minimum ministerial stipend of the day, and who died so soon after marriage, had left her with only the most exiguous of incomes, and since the course of training for the ministry required a minimum of seven years' attendance at the University. But she went forward in faith, no words being more often on her lips than 'The Lord will provide' and 'He will bless the house of Aaron'. She firmly believed that He would; and though she must often have been sorely worried, she not only kept her worries to herself but never allowed them to disturb either her inward peace or her outward demeanour. How she managed I have little notion, and I believe those of her contemporaries who knew her circumstances had even less. I can now see that there was little luxury in our household. I can remember that even in our teens a penny was still a precious coin. But as boys we had no awareness of being poorly off, nor can I believe that we ever lacked anything that we badly needed. *(The Theology of the Sacraments, pp 13-17)*

2 A CLASH OF CULTURES
by John Baillie

MY theological training began when, at the tender age of some five years, I was taught the first few responses of the Westminster Shorter Catechism. I was born in a Scottish Highland manse and all my early religious associations were with the more strictly Calvinistic type of Scottish Presbyterianism. The received creed was represented by the Westminster Confession of Faith, and my early boyhood was passed among men and women who knew and understood its elaborate doctrinal teaching through and through, and were well able to meet any difficulty which a boyish mind was likely to raise.

I have never since those days had the good fortune to live in a community that was, generally speaking, so well-informed in matters theological, so well acquainted with the contents of the Bible or so well able to explain and defend what it professed to believe. Not many systems of thought have been devised which (once certain initial premises are granted) hang together in so coherent a whole, or in which the vulnerable Achilles-heel is so hard to find.

But there were certain other features of this religion of the Scottish Highlands for which no mere study of its official symbols will prepare anyone who is a stranger to its inward life. There was here as deep and sincere a development of personal religion as could, perhaps, anywhere be pointed to in the Christian world. The practice of prayer, private, domestic and public, was given a primary place in the daily and weekly round and was a deep reality for men's thoughts. There was a strong evangelical note, so that one's mind was constantly being turned upon the necessity of regeneration, and yet any kind of sensational or over-emotional 'evangelistic' movement was looked at askance.

For never in any type of religion was there a greater sense of solemnity than in this one. Nowhere else, however imposing and fitting may have been the ritual, have I ever been so aware of the *mysterium tremendum* as in these rare celebrations of the Lord's Supper. Here, if ever, *das Numinose*, 'the sense of the holy', was found prevailing; the comparative rarity of the occasion giving to the sacramental feast that very same acuteness of emphasis which in another tradition (that I have since learned to prefer) is fostered rather by the opposite rule of frequency.

In recent days and in certain other parts of the world to which Scottish influence has penetrated, Presbyterianism has on occasion become a markedly unsacramental religion, the 'coming to the Lord's Table' being sometimes regarded as not very much more than a pleasant piece of old-fashioned sentiment and therefore an optional addition to one's central religious duties. Nothing, however, could be a greater departure from original Scottish religion as I knew it in my youth.

The whole year's religion then seemed to me to revolve round the two half-yearly celebrations, together with their attendant special services stretching from the 'Fast Day' on Thursday (when no business was done in the town and all the shops were shut) until the following Monday evening. The Scottish sacramental doctrine is a very 'high' one, though not in the sense of conformity to the too crude theory that developed within the Latin countries.

It was through associations formed at school that influences of another sort first began to play upon me, opening my eyes to certain spiritual deficiencies in this inherited system. I was fortunate in my masters. Since those days I have made acquaintance with a kind of schoolmaster who is greatly skilled in the mechanics of his profession and knows all there is to know (up to the very *dernier cri* in pedagogical theory) about how to teach – but who has little or nothing to impart! Of this kind of dominie it can truly be said that, if only he knew anything, his pupils would in time come to know it also.

My kind of dominie had, for the most part, an opposite combination of qualities and defects. My masters had minds richly stored with various knowledge, but this knowledge was more or less *thrown* at their pupils, to be taken or left according to one's tastes and abilities; and the wiles of modern educational strategy were left unpracticed. I think there were a large number of us with whom the method worked and who drew freely and eagerly upon the store thus set at our disposal.

* * *

I can remember how deeply I was moved in these days by our reading of the *Apology* and the *Phaedo* in the Greek class. That indeed, must be a common enough experience. There must be thousands who can recall what it was like to come upon these pages with a virgin mind. But I, at least, coming to them from my particular background, could not read Plato and Carlyle and Matthew Arnold without being, even then, aware of a slowly emerging intellectual problem. Here was a new world of thought opened out to me, a very different world from the austere Highland Calvinism of my immediate surroundings. To others of a widely different tradition one of these three writers, the dour Scot frae Ecclefechan, may seem to echo a typical calvinistic outlook, but it was of the difference – the difference that came to him so largely from the German and other romantics – and not of the resemblance that I was then aware. My difficulty was that through these new mentors I seemed to be becoming initiated into a certain region of truth and experience which could not easily be enclosed within the clearly defined frontiers of my traditional system.

('Confessions of a Transplanted Scot'
from V. Ferm (ed): *Contemporary American Theology:
Theological Autobiographics* (New York: 1933), pp 33-36)

3 Wrestling with Doubt
by John Baillie

I CAN remember, during my student years in Edinburgh, walking home one frosty midnight from a philosophical discussion on the existence of God, and stopping in my walk to gaze up into the starry sky. Into those deep immensities of space I hurled my despairing question, but it seemed to hit nothing, and no answer came back.

* * *

I believe a great many people have that sort of complaint to make against God. If God really exists, they say, why does He not declare Himself more plainly? Why does He not grant us a more unmistakable revelation? Why does He not make one quite certain sign, a sign that he who runs may read, a sign that would for ever put an end to doubt and afford us what we call 'fool-proof' evidence not only of His existence but of His will for mankind?

* * *

What I now realise very clearly, and am ready to confess, is that much of the trouble in the days when I could not hear God's voice was that I was not really listening. I was partly listening perhaps – giving, as it were, one ear to His commandments; but no promise is made in the Bible to those who partly listen, but only to those who hearken *diligently*. And why did I not thus hearken? It was that there were certain things I did not want to hear. We sometimes speak of people being 'conveniently deaf' to human communications, but there is such a thing also as being conveniently deaf towards God; and it is a malady that afflicts us all. There are certain things we just do not want to be told. They would be too inconvenient, too upsetting, too exacting. The readjustment they would involve would be too painful. They would commit us to tasks more difficult and troublesome than we desire

20

to undertake, or they would interfere with certain indulgences we have been allowing ourselves. The rich young man in the Gospels was so eager to get guidance from Jesus that he came to Him running (who says he was not eager?), asking what he must do to inherit eternal life. He had his guidance, but it was something he did not want to listen to: 'Sell whatsoever thou hast, and give to the poor. But when the young man heard that saying, he went away sorrowful: for he had great possessions' (Matthew 19:22; cf Luke 18:23). But he could never again complain of the lack of revelation.

Yet the matter is not always quite so simple as that. The obstacle of which I have spoken is the first that must be eliminated, and if it could be eliminated completely, the others would perhaps no longer give us pause. But other obstacles there are. I am indeed sure that much of my own trouble was of the same kind as the rich young man's; but it was also due in part to certain wrong-headed and illusory ideas that I had imbibed from the spirit of the age and from the philosophies that were then in vogue. Our intellectual sophistication is nowadays so great that it is difficult to achieve, or to recover, that naked contact of our minds with the confronting reality out of which true wisdom can alone be born. Jesus said, 'Except ye become as little children ...' (Matthew 18:3; cf Mark 10:15). He said also, 'I thank thee, O Father, Lord of heaven and earth, that thou hast hidden these things from the wise and learned, and hast revealed them to νηπιοις' – which we may perhaps translate as 'the innocent-minded' (Matthew 11:25; Luke 10:21). Only the innocent and childlike mind can hearken diligently.

There are thus two questions which I would put to those (and first to myself) who complain that they are aware of no divine self-disclosure, or that God does not speak to them more plainly. First, *Are you sure there is not something which He is plainly saying to you, and to which you are not giving ear?* Are you really prepared to hear whatever God may have in mind to say to you, no matter what it may turn out to be? Can you honestly say that there is no voice now seeking to make itself heard, and to which you are not attending – perhaps pretending to yourself that you do not hear it? It may be a sense of dissatisfaction with your present way of living, or with some one particular thing in your life, and you are half-unconsciously suppressing it. Or it may be some positive task that is calling you, and you are as it were stopping your ears, because the task is distasteful to you. But it is God who is speaking. That is how He always speaks. That is how revelation always comes.

*   *   *

The second question which I would put is this: *If you have listened, have you obeyed?* In the Bible that is always part of the condition: 'If thou wilt diligently hearken to the voice of the Lord thy God ... and wilt give ear to his commandments, and keep all his statutes ....' That seems to mean that we can receive no further revelation until we have not only hearkened to, but also acted upon, such revelation as we have already received. Nor do I see that we have any right to grumble at such a dispensation, if indeed it exists. What right have we to ask for more light when we are not using the light we already have? It may be that we do not know what we ask, when we ask for a full revelation of God. I can remember being pulled up by a sentence written by the Blessed Henry Suso in AD 1335: 'Let not him ask after what is highest in doctrine who yet stands on what is lowest in a good life' (Heinrich Suso, *Das Büchlein der ewigen Weisheit*, chapter xxi). Yet here we are, clamouring for the mystery of ultimate reality to be laid bare to us, and not facing up to the little sample of reality that stares us full in the face – the realities, it may be, of the family relationships in our own home! This one bit of God's will for us we do at least know, this immediate duty that lies so close to our hand. But we do not take to it very kindly. We find it harsh and unwelcome enough. Is it not probable, then, that anything like a full revelation would quite crush us – and quite blind us. 'Our God,' as we read both in the Old Testament and in the New, 'is a consuming fire' (Deuteronomy 4:24; Hebrews 12:29):

No angel in the sky
Can fully bear that sight.

~ Matthew Bridges: 'Crown Him with Many Crowns' ~

Surely, then, we had better learn to adjust ourselves to the more commonplace demands of our domestic situation before we enquire after that before which the cherubim veil their faces:

We need not bid, for cloistered cell,
Our neighbour and our work farewell,
Nor strive to wind ourselves too high
For sinful man beneath the sky;

The trivial round, the common task,
Will furnish all we ought to ask.

~ John Keble: 'O timely happy!' ~

We must therefore accept the second condition also: before asking for what we do not hear, we must obey what we do hear. We may remind ourselves of the precept which was 'of invaluable service' to Thomas Carlyle when he found himself in what he calls 'the fixed tartarean dark' of mid-nineteenth-century unbelief: 'Do the duty which lies nearest to thee, which thou knowest to be a duty. Thy second duty will already have become clearer' (Thomas Carlyle, *Sartor Resartus*, 'The Everlasting Yea').

(The Idea of Revelation in Recent Thought, pp 138-146)

*   *   *

After taking his degree Donald entered New College, Edinburgh and submitted himself to the regular four years' course of theological study in preparation for the ministry. His struggle for faith was now measurably eased, but certainly not yet a thing of the past. Indeed it was never for him completely a thing of the past. Even in his latest years he had periods of depression, in which life seemed to be emptied of its divine meaning. He was in the poorest possible health then, a martyr to a long-standing asthmatic condition, and the depression was physical as well as mental. He would put to himself and to me the question as to whether the extreme bodily lassitude was the cause or the result, or merely the accompaniment, of the darkness of soul. But one thing was always clear to him – that without God and Christ human life was without significance of any kind, devoid of all interest. He would say, 'When the darkness is on me, I walk down the street, and see people walking aimlessly about, and shops and cars and a few dogs, and it all seems to mean nothing and to matter not at all!' It was Pascal's *misère de l'homme sans Dieu*. Blessedly, such periods of depression were seldom of long duration, and certainly (whatever may be thought about cause and effect) they were always associated with the ebbings of his physical resources. Moreover, this whole side of his experience undoubtedly enabled him to enter most sympathetically and most helpfully into the like experience of a large number of students and others who sought his counsel. Only three or four days before his death, as I travelled to his bedside, a young sick-nurse who sat facing me in the railway compartment told me she was on her way home for a long rest necessitated by her nervous condition; and when I asked her if she knew what brought it on, she answered, 'There has recently been a large number of deaths in our nursing-home, some of them terribly distressing, and I can't stand it now that I've ceased to believe in God'. I recounted this to Donald, and through the fabric of his oxygen tent he said to me, 'How many people feel like that, and how many have spoken just like that to me!'

(The Theology of the Sacraments, pp 21-22)

(B) *God*

1 THINKING THE TRINITY
by Donald Baillie

In the name of the Father, and of the Son, and of the Holy Ghost.
~ Matthew 28:19 ~

ON this Trinity Sunday I wish to speak about the doctrine of the Trinity. That sounds formidable and uninviting. But surely we ought not to shirk the task of understanding it. We sing 'God in three Persons, blessed Trinity'. What do we mean? Perhaps we couldn't say. Perhaps we are just mystified. Perhaps this doctrine of three in one, of Trinity in Unity, conveys nothing to our minds but the sense of sheer mystery.

Well, even that is something. The sense of mystery is quite wholesome, in all our thoughts of God, for no human mind can comprehend Him. But mystery is not enough. We need a positive God. And I believe we can find the whole Christian Gospel summed up in this mysterious doctrine, of three Persons, Father, Son and Holy Spirit, in one God. Let us try.

(1) First of all: *One God.* That is very important. It is part of the good news. When Christianity first went out into the pagan world with its Gospel, many people were tired of the old religions, and this was one of the really splendid things about the new Gospel: that instead of a whole host of gods it offered them ONE true God. To us that is so familiar that we don't realize what good news it is. But we would realize it if we had been brought up on a religion which had many gods. You can read in missionary books today of how it comes as a tremendous relief to heathen people when they learn from Christian missionaries that, instead of a whole host of gods and spirits to be propitiated, there is one great God over all, and that they have to do with Him alone.

A famous divine of the middle ages said wittily that the Devil was the first grammarian, when he taught men to give a plural to the word God. It ought not to have a plural. For if you have more than one God, you never know where you are. To put it into modern terms: if you divide your heart between different loyalties, if you idolize many things, if you believe not only in Providence, but also in blind Fate, and in lucky numbers and charms and mascots, and in the Almighty dollar above all, then life is distracted, your heart is torn asunder, because you have too many gods. Anything more than One is too many. For there is only one true God. That is what the great prophets of Israel told the world, when the world had gone astray after many gods. They said: All that is based on a lie, and a tragic lie, which destroys all justice and truth and trust among men, and turns the universe into a chaos of conflicting forces and claims. It is a lie. And the truth is far better. It is the good news of One God who governs the whole world in righteousness and mercy; and to trust in Him alone is salvation. 'Look unto me and be ye saved, all the ends of the earth. For I am God, and there is none else.'

That was something gained once for all in the education of the human race, and never to be lost or forgotten: the good news that *God is One.* That is fundamental.

Why wasn't that enough? Why did Christianity have to go on to say something more, and something so complicated and mysterious – that in the Unity there is a Trinity? It was not because God, as it were, dropped down from heaven a ready-made doctrine for our acceptance, a mathematical doctrine of three in one and one in three. That is not how God reveals His truth, and if He did, it wouldn't help us much, but would simply leave us guessing. Why then did Christianity have to go on from the One God to the Three-in-One?

Well, it was because something happened, and then something else happened. There were two new facts of history and experience. Let us think what they were.

(2) *The fact of Jesus Christ.* About nineteen centuries ago there appeared among the Jews in Palestine a new religious leader, a working-man called Jesus. His career did not last long, for He got into trouble with the authorities and was condemned to death. But on His followers He had made such an impression that they

were faced with a quite new task of explanation. Who and what was this Jesus? He had come into their lives and made everything different. He had brought God into their lives in a way they had never known before, and He had brought forgiveness and joy and power and victory over sin and death. He had been put to death Himself, yet somehow they were convinced that His very death had been the greatest victory of all, reconciling sinners to God; and to complete the victory, He had risen from the dead.

But how could Jesus accomplish all that? What was the meaning of it? The only possible meaning, they felt, was this: that God was in Christ. This was not just Jesus of Nazareth. Somehow it was God. Yet how could that be? Was Jesus simply identical with God? Was 'Jesus' just another name for God? No, that could not be quite right. For Jesus was a real man, in both body and mind. Jesus talked about God, and He used to pray to God; and He was tempted, as all men are, and He suffered pain, and then He died on the Cross. But not one of these things could be said without qualification about God the Father Almighty.

Then was Jesus a kind of second God, alongside of God the Father? No, that was impossible for there could not be two Gods. God is eternally one. Then was Jesus a kind of demi-god, something between God and Man, half and half? No, that would be of no use, for then you would lose both the divine and the human. Jesus would be neither God nor Man, but a mythological figure, like the demi-gods that were so plentiful in other religions. That was not a bit like the Christ they had known: and what could such a figure do for man's salvation? It was not a demi-god, but the very God Himself, that they needed and that they found in Jesus.

What then were they to say about it? Well, they had to go on and find new expressions, and say things that had never been said about God before. They said that God became incarnate in Jesus; and yet somehow God did not become wholly, absolutely incarnate, for they knew that God also remained all the time the eternal invisible omnipotent God in Heaven. They had to make further distinctions. So they said it was the Word of God that became incarnate. 'The Word was made flesh.' But there was another expression still more natural. Jesus Himself had continually spoken of God as His Father, and He had a deep continual sense of sonship to God. So they began to speak of the Son of God. It was not God the Father, but God the Son, that was incarnate and became Man. They did not mean that there were two Gods, or that God the Father and God the Son were two quite separate individuals like a human father and son, for there can only be one God. Really they meant something they could not adequately put into words at all. For in Jesus Christ something new and tremendous had come into their lives, and it stretched all their thoughts of God to find new expressions. So they came to speak of the Father and the Son; and even if they couldn't quite explain it or think it out, it was at the very heart of their faith.

It was all because of this tremendous new fact in their experience – the fact of Jesus Christ.

(3) *The fact of Pentecost.* But something else happened, and there is another historic fact that went to the making of the doctrine of the Trinity. We may indicate it by the word Pentecost.

Remember that the disciples of Jesus had their Master with them in the flesh for only a few brief years, and that no other Christians ever since have had that experience at all. To the disciples it was an infinitely marvellous experience. Jesus had brought God into their lives. And if they ever faced the thought that He might be taken away from them suddenly, the prospect of such a bereavement was overwhelming. How could they ever get on at all without Him? Their whole faith in God would collapse.

But if a few months after the departure of Jesus you had asked these disciples whether they missed their Master very badly, and whether they had lost God out of their lives altogether, they would have replied with a joyful and unanimous NO. Indeed they would have told you that somehow the Divine Presence was far more real and powerful in their lives now than ever it had been while their Master was with them in the flesh. It was expedient, they now saw, that their Master should have departed in order that this new experience should come to them.

There was one great day in particular when the experience came home to them. It was on the date of a Jewish festival called Pentecost. The disciples and some others who had become

Christians were assembled in a large room in Jerusalem for fellow-ship and prayer, when they had a marvellous experience, an over-whelming sense of the presence and power of God. And now they were quite sure that they had lost neither God nor Jesus. Jesus seemed nearer than ever. Though they could not see Him with their own eyes, it was only now that they began really to under-stand Him. And God had come into their lives as never before – far more marvellously than even while their Master was on earth – so that now they could go anywhere and witness for Him. Moreover, they very soon found that this great experience need not be confined to those who had known Jesus in the flesh. This was a thing that could happen to anybody anywhere, through the story of Jesus. A new power was abroad in the world; and wherever the apostles went with the message, the new thing kept on happening, in the lives of all sorts of people, just as it had come to the apostles themselves on the Day of Pentecost.

What was it? Was it simply the Jesus they had known, now come back to them unseen? Yes, in a way. They did sometimes speak of it as the presence of Christ. And yet it was not just the same. It was something greater and more universal than what they had known when Jesus was with them in the flesh – the same, yet different, deepened and widened and freed from all limitations of space and time. Was it, then, simply the presence of the Eternal God himself? Yes, and yet it was something new, something beyond what men had ever known of God before, something that could not have happened but for the work of Jesus.

What was it? How were they to define it? Well, they remem-bered that in the Old Testament, whenever such a power came into the lives of certain outstanding and exceptional men, it was described as the Spirit of the Lord coming upon them. They remembered also that a prophet called Joel had once foretold the coming of a time when the Spirit of God would be poured out, not on a few exceptional people, but on all sorts of ordinary men and women. And they remembered that their own Master Jesus had said God would give his Holy Spirit to those who asked Him. So now on the Day of Pentecost they said: 'This is what Joel predicted. This is what Jesus promised. And God our Heavenly Father, who came to us in his son Jesus, is with us now, and for evermore, in this new and wonderful way, through His Holy Spirit.'

And that is how Christians have come to speak of Father, Son and Holy Spirit, One God.

Can you see now why I said that the doctrine of the Trinity sums up the whole Christian Gospel? I began by saying that it is good news to learn that God is One. But, as you see, there is still better news in the message that the One God is Father, Son and Holy Spirit, when you really understand it. Of course to say merely 'three in one and one in three' – that in itself means nothing. But when it comes at the end of the story, it tells you everything. It tells you of what God is, in His eternal and infinite love; and of what God did in Jesus Christ for our salvation; and of what God does still today, dwelling with us as truly as He dwelt among men nineteen centuries ago, and the same for evermore. So to those who know the story, the doctrine of the Trinity sums up the whole Gospel. And the Church never tires of singing in gratitude: 'Glory be to the Father, and to the Son, and to the Holy Ghost: as it was in the beginning, is now, and ever shall be, world without end.'

(To Whom Shall We Go?, pp 73-79)

2 OUR KNOWLEDGE OF GOD
by John Baillie

I BELIEVE the view to be capable of defence that no one of the four subjects of our knowledge – ourselves, our fellows, the corporeal world, and God – is ever presented to us except in conjunction with all three of the others. Here, however, we need only concern ourselves with the fact that God does not present Himself to us except in conjunction with the presence of our fellows and of the corporeal world.

Taking the second point first, it seems plain that the consciousness of God is never given save in conjunction with the consciousness of things. We do not know God through the world, but we know Him with the world; and in knowing Him with the world, we know Him as its ground. Nature is not an argument for God, but it is a sacrament of Him. Just as in the sacrament of Holy Communion the Real Presence of Christ is given (if the Lutheran phrase may here be used without prejudice) 'in, with and under' the bread and wine, so in a wider sense the whole corporeal world may become sacramental to us of the presence of the Triune God .... No writer has done more to clarify our thought on this matter than Baron von Hugel. 'Necessity of the Thing-element in Religion' is not only the title of a section in his greatest work (*The Mystical Element in Religion*, 2nd edition, vol ii, pp 372ff) but a constant theme in all his works. 'Spirit' he tells us, 'is awakened on occasion of Sense' (*Essays and Addresses*, 2nd series, p 246). The knowledge of God, he insists, is not during this life given to us in its isolated purity, but only through 'the 'the humiliations of the material order'. (See the chapter on 'The Natural Order' in M Nedoncelle's *Baron Friedrich von Hugel*.) The knowledge of God which we have on earth is of a kind that we cannot conceive to exist apart from some knowledge of things.

But it is equally certain that all our knowledge of God is given us 'in, with and under' our knowledge of one another. This means, first, that the knowledge of God is withholden from those who keep themselves aloof from the *service* of their fellows. It means that 'He that loveth not knoweth not God' (I John 4:8), whereas 'If we love one another, God dwelleth in us' (I John 4:12). And this is indeed a blessed provision by which God makes my knowledge of Himself pass through my brother's need. It means, second, that only when I am in *fellowship* with my fellow men does the knowledge of God come to me individually. It means the necessity of the Church and the rejection of religious individualism. It gives the true sense of the Cyprianic formula, *extra ecclesiam nulla salus*. 'For where two or three are gathered together in my name, there am I in the midst of them' (Matthew 18:20). Such was the promise; and its fulfilment came when the disciples 'were all with one accord in one place' and the Spirit 'sat upon each of them' (Acts 2:1-3). It means, third, the necessity of history. There is a necessary historical element in all religion, for we know of no religion that is not dependent on tradition; but Christianity is plainly an historical religion in the fullest possible sense. The Christian knowledge of God is not given to any man save in conjunction with the telling of an 'old, old story'. Therefore it means, lastly, the necessity of Christ, God incarnate in the flesh. 'For there is one God, and one mediator between God and men, the man Christ Jesus; who gave Himself a ransom for all, to be testified in due time' (I Timothy 2:5-6). The service of others, the fellowship with others, and the historical tradition in which I stand are all media that lead me to the Mediator, and the Mediator leads me to God. And all this mediation is part of God's gracious purpose in refusing to unite me to Himself without at the same time uniting me to my fellow men – in the making it impossible for me to obey either of the two great commandments without at the same time obeying the other.

*　　*　　*

Clearly, then, the immediacy of God's presence to our souls is a mediated immediacy. But I must now do what I can to resolve the apparent self-contradictoriness of this phrase.

What I must do is to ask myself how the knowledge of God first came to me. And here I can only repeat what was said in the opening pages of this book: unless my analysis of my memory is altogether at fault, the knowledge of God first came to me in the form of an awareness that I was 'not my own' but one under authority, one who 'owed' something, one who 'ought' to be something which he was not. But whence did this awareness come to me? Certainly it did not come 'out of the blue'. I heard no voice from the skies. No, it came, without a doubt, from what I may call the spiritual climate of the home into which I was born. It came from my parents' walk and conversation. At the beginning it may have been merely the consciousness of a conflict between my mother's will and my own, between what I desired and what she desired of me. Yet I cannot profess to remember a time when it was merely that. I cannot remember a time when I did not already dimly know that what opposed my own wilfulness was something much more than mere wilfulness on my mother's part. I knew she had a right to ask of me what she did; which is the same as to say that I knew that what she asked of me was right and that my contrary desire was wrong. I knew, therefore, that my mother's will was not the ultimate source of the authority which she exercised over me. For it was plain that she herself was under that same authority. Indeed, it was not only from my parents' specific demands on me that this sense of authority came to me but from the way they themselves lived. Clearly they, too, were under orders, and under essentially the same orders. I cannot remember a time when I did not already know that what my parents demanded of me and what they knew to be demanded of themselves were in the last resort one and the same demand, however different might be its detailed application to our different situations. I cannot remember a time when I did not know that my parents and their household were part of a wider community which was under the same single authority. Nor, again, can I recall a time when I did not know that this authority was closely bound up with, and indeed seemed to emanate from, a certain story. As far back as I can remember anything, my parents and my nurses were already speaking to me of Abraham and Isaac and Jacob, of Moses and David, of God's covenant with the Israelites and of their journey through the wilderness, of the culmination of the story in the coming of Jesus Christ, God's only Son, whom he sent to earth to suffer and die for our salvation; and then of the apostles and martyrs and saints and 'Scots worthies' whose golden deeds brought the story down to very recent days. And I knew that that story was somehow the source of the authority with which I was confronted. I could not hear a Bible story read without being aware that in it I was somehow being confronted with a solemn presence that had in it both sweetness and rebuke. Nor do I remember a day when I did not already dimly know that this presence was God.

It was, then, through the media of my boyhood's home, the Christian community of which it formed a part, and the 'old, old story' from which that community drew its life, that God first revealed Himself to me. This is simple matter of fact. But what I take to be matter of fact in it is not only that God used these media but that in using them he actually did reveal Himself to *my* soul.

(*Our Knowledge of God*, pp 187-184)

3 ON GOD AND GOODNESS
by Donald Baillie

THE view of faith to which we are being led may seem to imply that every man who is loyal to his moral convictions has religious faith in his heart, or at least that every such man is bound to attain to such a faith as time goes on: and this appears impossible to reconcile with the familiar facts of modern life. How can we maintain that the moral life and religious faith are thus inseparable? Are there not in the modern world many good men, of pure and earnest and self-sacrificing moral life, who are entirely devoid of any positive religious beliefs? Have we not in this very study seen it to be a common thing for moral convictions and loyalties to remain unshaken when all religious belief has gone? And it seems impossible even to maintain that loyalty to one's moral convictions always leads in the long run to religious belief: many great names of the modern world will spring up in the reader's mind to contradict that notion.

Yet there is in the consciousness of the modern world a deep strain of wisdom which tells us that every good man somehow has the root of the matter in him, the germ of religious faith, even if he is hindered from the realization of it by the necessity of rejecting false formulations with which faith has come to be associated. This is the truth which Tennyson expressed classically when he said that 'There lives more faith in honest doubt ... than in half the creeds'. But even the naive religious mind is aware of it. The present writer can remember the comment made by a quite unsophisticated religious woman in speaking of the local atheist, who was really a good sort of man: 'He *thinks* he's an atheist, but he's better than his creed.' The implication is that no good man is really an atheist, though he may call himself such. Many illustrations of this insight might be given from modern literature. Dr L. P. Jacks has a story of a village cobbler who 'spent his breath in proving that God did not exist, but spent his life in proving that he did'. Another perfect illustration may be found in that great novel which we have already found so illuminating, Tolstoy's *Anna*

Karenin. Levin was 'an unbeliever', and had been one for many years, overcome by the scientific difficulties which stood in the way of religious belief, and always unhappy about it. But in a moment of great anxiety he suddenly caught himself ejaculating a prayer. 'At that instant he knew that all his doubts, even the impossibility of believing with his reason, of which he was aware in himself, did not in the least hinder his turning to God. All of that now floated out of his soul like dust.' Again, his devoted and religious young wife did not worry at all about what he called his unbelief, though she knew that all unbelievers would be damned. She had been terribly distressed when he told her that in former days he had been guilty of moral lapses; but now 'she thought with a smile of his unbelief, and told herself that he was absurd'. 'He an unbeliever indeed! With his heart, his dread of offending any one, even a child! Everything for others, nothing for himself' (*Anna Karenin*, translated by C. Garnett, vol ii). She felt that a good man like him could not *really* be an unbeliever, whatever his intellectual position might be. What could unbelief mean in such a man, who obviously believed in those absolute values which are one with the Kingdom of God? And when Levin did eventually find faith, as we saw, it seemed to him but the discovery of something which had been in him all the time, and on which he had been living, though he had not realized it. 'Thou wouldst not be seeking Me,' said the divine voice to Pascal, 'if thou didst not possess Me' (Pascal, *Pensées* (Brunschvieg), vii, p 555).

(*Faith in God*, pp 182-184)

ON GOD AND GOODNESS
by John Baillie

How can faith in God thus be a natural accompaniment of loyalty to our values?

The answer is that faith in God naturally accompanies such loyalty because it is a thing that is itself very closely akin to it. Indeed we may say that to believe in duty and to believe in God are not, for the man of faith, two different beliefs, but only one belief. To believe in God is, at least in its beginnings, hardly more than a deeper way of believing in duty. What happens is simply that to the seeker, in the course of his loyal striving to do the right and eschew the wrong, and to do 'the utmost for the highest', there comes – sometimes with the light of a sudden revelation, but more often slowly and gradually – the realisation of a new and deeper meaning that there is in duty and goodness. He has been believing all along that goodness and love and honour are the things that matter most in all the world, and he has been seeking these things with a single-hearted devotedness. But now there grows up in his mind something like a conviction that these things are the very pillars on which the world is built. For how could they matter as they do, if they be not central to the System of Things in which he has his humble part to play? All along he has been believing that there is laid upon him an absolute obligation to do what is right and to follow the narrow and difficult way of duty and of selfless service. But now he comes to feel, in a clear and explicit way, that it is nothing less than the hidden nature of things that is laying this obligation upon him. For how can he be obliged to do the right if, in the last resort, the Universe does not care whether he do the right or the wrong? 'I *must* seek the highest,' he says, and there is nothing of which he is more sure; but whence can that *must* derive, if not from the nature of things? Why must he, if he be part and parcel of a System for which the highest is as the lowest and the lowest as the highest?

I do not mean to suggest, of course, that the ordinary man in whose soul faith comes to birth ever asks himself these questions in a self-conscious way. What actually happens in the large majority of cases is no doubt simply that, without his knowing it, duty begins to wear a new aspect to him and to acquire a new significance. Perhaps, most of all, it is a sense of the *purpose* of things that comes to him. He begins to feel that he was *meant* to seek the highest, that to this end was he born; and above all there grows upon him the feeling that in seeking it he is fulfilling his appointed destiny and putting himself in line with Something greater than himself. The truth is that no man to whom there comes the strong sense that in doing his duty he is doing what is *required* of him is far from the true faith. Was not the very nerve-centre of the faith of Jesus Christ himself just this sense of Higher Appointment that accompanied him in all his work; the sense of being sent; the sense that, in doing what he had to do, he was doing the will of him that sent him? Such a sense is the most blessed accompaniment to which any man can work. Perhaps it is a thing that comes, in some measure, and sooner or later, to all good workmen. And it is what we mean by faith in God.

(The Roots of Religion in the Human Soul, pp 221-225)

4 The Shema
by John Baillie

MAN is a talking animal. A poet, watching the swallows gathering in the sky, may write that 'The pilgrims of the year waxed very loud, in multitudinous chatterings', but no other animal is such a chatterbox as man. Sometimes, when travelling in a country whose language I did not understand, I have sat in an inn or railway compartment or wandered through a crowded market-place, when every tongue seemed to be going at lightning speed, everybody apparently trying to talk everybody else down; and I've wondered what on earth they could possibly be finding to say to one another. And it would seem that the more primitive the community, the more unimpeded is the flow of words. Savages chatter almost unceasingly. Silence is not primitive, but rather a characteristic of complex and sophisticated civilizations, being due either to diplomacy, as in the case of Count Moltke who was said to have the gift of being 'silent in seven languages', or to social embarrassment – though in this case we can always, in this country at least, save the situation by falling back upon our changeable weather.

What do we talk about, you and I, when we sit at table or by the fireside with our families, or when we go out walking with them? We always find something to say, and perhaps we are inclined to think that it does not very much matter what it is.

Conversation is a social function which keeps us in friendly touch with each other, no matter what may be the topics discussed. It may only be sport or the increased cost of living or the day's news or the latest movie or, as George Crabbe put it long ago,

> *Intrigues half-gathered, conversation-scraps,*
> *Kitchen-cabals, and nursery-mishaps …*

but it all helps, as it were, to lubricate our human and family relationships and keep them sweet, if it is carried on pleasantly and with good humour.

Yes, but the first question I want to put is whether conversation really *can* be kept sweet, if it remains on that superficial level. It is remarkable how easy we human beings find it to pick a quarrel with one another. Even the smallest of small talk will provide plenty of opportunity for it. Some little devil always seems to be listening in at even our most casual conversations, and it is seldom very long before he finds an opportunity of sowing discord. And to allow one devil in is to allow a whole crowd of them – the devils of bitterness and malice and jealousy, the devils of untruthfulness and slander and back-biting. St Paul knew all about it when he wrote to Timothy about 'strifes of words, whereof cometh envy, strife, railings, evil surmisings, perverse disputings'.

I am sure that if we are honest with ourselves we shall all have to confess to the very great difficulty in keeping these devils at bay. The first little devil makes his entry so unobtrusively that we are far from suspecting the legion at his heels. What is it another poet says?

> *'Who knocks so loud?' 'A little lonely sin.'*
> *'Enter,' I answered; and all hell was in.*

We just can't resist that barbed word, that little dig. It is such a little dig, but if it pricks and is resented, then we can't help remarking that apparently 'the cap fits'; and that lets in a whole crowd of demons at a rush. While our own shortcomings are hidden from us, the shortcomings of others stand out so clearly that we can't help drawing their attention to them. Of course they pay back in kind, and since it is even more difficult to refrain from self-defence than it originally was to refrain from launching the attack, we soon find ourselves in the thick of battle.

It is in this way that family relations are poisoned. Our sentimentalities about the joys of the fireside circle and 'home, sweet home' are apt to be considerably chastened by a study of the Divorce Court proceedings, and yet the vast majority of these family tragedies seem to take their rise in just such trivial bickerings. But what is true of the family is true of every other kind of social group. Nor must I, as one whose whole life has been spent in colleges, exempt the Senior Common Rooms of our universities; for I am ashamed to confess that even the shabbiest of household devils seem to find no special difficulty in slipping into them. And what of the wider circles of community? What above all of the family of nations? Don't some of the disputes at the council tables of the United Nations read exactly like the disputes round the dinner table in many a private household? It is not a different set of devils, but precisely the same set, that builds so many barriers between husbands and wives, and that forged the 'iron curtain' now dividing Eastern Europe from the West.

What then can we do about it? How are we to keep these devils out? The answer is that they cannot be kept out while our relationships with one another, our walk and conversation with one another, remain on that superficial level. Our human predicament is so desperately serious, and our human nature so desperately prone to wickedness, that common life cannot be kept sweet so long as it remains trivial. It is only by going deep down to the heart of things that we can find a solidarity strong enough to overcome the surface tensions; and the deep heart of things is God. Only by together laying hold of the divine unity, only by grounding ourselves on the knowledge that 'the Lord our God is one Lord', can we ever master the things that divide us. We can never shut the little devils out unless we let the great God in.

Now listen again to our text. Remember that these are the words which, according to the Book of Deuteronomy, Moses spoke to the Israelites as they were about to enter the promised land of

Canaan after their long desert wandering. They were going to adjust themselves now to the humdrum of a steady pastoral existence after the unsettled nomadic life to which for so long they had been used, and their society would now be open to new temptations. So Moses said to them:

> *Hear O Israel: The Lord our God is one Lord: and thou shalt love the Lord thy God with all thine heart, and with all thy soul, and with all thy might. And these words, which I command thee this day, shall be in thy heart: and thou shalt teach them diligently unto thy children, and shalt talk of them when thou sittest in thine house, and when thou walkest by the way, and when thou liest down and when thou risest up. And thou shalt bind them for a sign upon thine hand, and they shall be as frontlets between thine eyes. And thou shalt write them upon the posts of thine house, and on thy gates.*

When you read that, do you wonder that even in this modern day we must continue to go back to the ancient East, to these rude tribesmen of three thousand years ago, and to these ancient Hebrew scriptures, for the solution of our most urgent problems? How these words touch the very heart of the matter! The only way, so these rude tribesmen are told, to keep their life sweet in their new surroundings, the only way to keep the legion of Canaanite devils out, is constantly to stay themselves upon the unity of God, and to love the one God with all their heart and soul and might. And you will notice that they are given specific guidance as to their *conversation*: 'thou shalt talk of these things when thou sittest in thy house, and when thou walkest by the way, and when thou liest down, and when thou risest up' – not just in an occasional theological debate, which is so apt to become academic and unreal, but in the ordinary small talk of every day. 'And thou shalt teach them diligently to thy children' – ah! that was a very important part of it. It makes us ask ourselves what kind of upbringing the little ones are receiving in many homes today. What teaching are they getting, and above all what example are they being shown? What is being laid up in their young hearts? What things have their young ears sometimes to listen to?

'And thou shalt bind these words for a sign upon thine hand, and they shall be as frontlets between thine eyes. And thou shalt write them upon the posts of thine house, and on thy gates.' The Hebrew people came to take these instructions very literally – probably more literally than was originally meant. 'Hear, O Israel': the Hebrew word for 'hear' is *shema*; so the words which follow came to be known as the *Shema*, which to this day is recited as part of the service in every Jewish synagogue. And at morning and evening prayer every Jewish male still wears the two phylacteries as they came to be called, one between his eyebrows and the other tied round his left arm, with these words written on them; and every observant Jewish house has a little box, containing a scrap of parchment inscribed with the same words, fixed to the post of the door.

The *Shema* is the very centre of Jewish piety, and goes far to explain the marvellous strength of Hebrew family life and the solidarity of the Hebrew community throughout the ages. There is more in our Christian creed than the *Shema,* but the *Shema* is a vital part of it; and we Scots, no less than the Hebrews, owe the strength of our family and community life to its having been anciently built on this foundation. What was the talk like in the Christian homes of Scotland's past? What was it like in the household of my own youth and in the other households I used to visit? We talked of fun and games and books and the happy trivialities of school and home; yes, but it was always against the background of something sterner and more profound. Our parents diligently taught us the commandments of God, often leading us back to them as we sat in the house or walked by the way, and always – *always* – when we lay down or when we rose up. Though not literally, yet none the less truly, they were bound for a sign upon our hands and as frontlets between our eyes; and they were written upon the posts and on the gates of the house where I was born. What after all would our history have been apart from this? What has Scottish history to show the world that was really independent of it? We have other reasons for reading the history of Greece and of Rome, but what other reason have we for reading either the history of Israel or the history of Scotland? I think Scotland must confess with St Paul, 'He that glorieth, let him glory in the Lord'. When walking in the island of Lewis a few years ago, I happened to stop for a moment at the open window of a shed where herrings were being packed. Immediately inside the window was a machine that seemed to split and clean the herrings, and pack them into cases, all in a single operation. A young woman was tending the machine, and when she looked at me I said, 'That is a wonderful machine'. 'Aye, sir,' she answered, 'the works of man are wonderful, but not so wonderful as the works of God!' Well, when I want to boast about Scotland, I tell a few stories like that; for not in every part of the world would I have received such an answer.

Are we doing for our children of the rising generation what our fathers and mothers did for us? Are we keeping this tradition green? Times change, and the superficialities of life change with them. The topics of conversation round the dinner-table are now very different from what they were in my youth. But the ultimate issues of life remain quite unchanged. 'Other foundation can no man lay than that is laid, which is Jesus Christ.' Most of us know that, under God, we owe everything to the influences that were brought to bear on us in early life. I have heard a man of my own generation exclaim in the course of a discussion, 'Whatever you may say about Christianity, it made my mother what she was'. Will our children be likely to say a thing like that about us? I can imagine no greater service we could render to Christ than that twenty or thirty years hence our children should be fortified in their allegiance to Him as often as they remember how *we* were enabled by His grace.

Yet let us not think in this matter of Scotland only. The old national frontiers count for so much less than they used to do. The world, whether we like it or not, is more and more developing into a single interdependent community; and the failure to recognise this, or the attempt to erect any kind of iron curtain between the nations, can only lead to disaster. Moreover, I believe this to be a cause for Christian rejoicing. The world is destined to become one just because God is one – because, as the *Shema* says, 'The Lord our God is one Lord'. Yet I think we all know that this one world will prove quite unmanageably large and cumbrous, if it does not ground itself also on the rest of the *Shema,* 'Thou shalt love the Lord thy God with all thine heart and soul and might'. The great peril of our time lies in the fact that the secular unity of our world is threatening to outstrip its spiritual unity. If no single nation has ever succeeded in holding together on the basis of merely economic or utilitarian interest, if every stable society known to history has owed its stability to the presence among its members of some common spiritual outlook, what hope is there for our United Nations, if it is to have no profound basis of that kind at all? That is why you and I must cease to be parochial, and give at least as much thought and prayer, as much time and as much money, to the the task of world-evangelisation as to the maintenance of the Christian traditions of our own beloved land.

(A Reasoned Faith, pp 44-51)

(C) *Jesus Christ*

1 THE PARADOX OF GRACE AND THE TWO NATURES OF CHRIST
by Donald Baillie

LET us try to trace more fully the connection and analogy between what I have called the paradox of grace and the paradox of the Incarnation.

Let us begin with the witness of the New Testament. It is plain that we find in the New Testament both the very highest claims for the divine revelation in Jesus and the very frankest recognition that He was a man. How far can we also find these two related to each other in a way that reminds us of the paradox by which a Christian says: 'I, … yet not I, but God'?

Throughout the story we get the impression of one who, with all His high claims, kept thinking far less of Himself than of the Father. Even in Him – or should we say, supremely in Him? –

self-consciousness was swallowed up in His deep and humble and continual consciousness of God. When He worked cures, it was to His heavenly Father that He looked up for aid, and it was to God rather than to Himself that He expected people to give the glory when they were cured (Mark 7:34; 5:19; Luke 17:18). As regards goodness, He was not conscious of possessing it Himself independently, but looked away from Himself to God for it. When once a man addressed him as 'Good Master', He replied: 'Why do you call me good? No one is good except God (Mark 10:17f). If we take the reply seriously, we shall surely find in it the supreme instance of that peculiar kind of humility which Christianity brought into the world. It was not self-depreciation: it was rather a complete absence of the kind of self-consciousness which makes a man think of his own degree of merit, and a dominating sense of dependence on God. The man in whom God was incarnate would claim nothing for Himself as a man, but ascribed all glory to God.

It hardly needs to be said the New Testament is conscious of a great gulf between what Christ is and what we are even when we are His people; and to some it may seem that this should exclude all analogy between his experience of God and ours. Especially it may occur to some that experience of the *grace* of God belongs to sinful men and does not enter at all into the mystery of divine Incarnation.

It is relevant, however, to remember that the New Testament, while it speaks of the grace of God as given to Christ, speaks much more of the grace of Christ as given to us. And that indicates exactly the relation between His experience of God and ours, as conceived in the New Testament. Ours depends upon His. If God in some measure lives and acts in us, it is because first, and without measure, He lived and acted in Christ. And thus, further, the New Testament tends sometimes to say that as God dwells in Christ so Christ dwells in us. St Paul can express the paradox of grace by saying: 'I live; and yet no longer I, but *Christ* liveth in me' (Galatians 2:20); as he can say to Christians: 'You are of Christ, and Christ is of God' (I Corinthians 3:23). But that is only a part of the truth, and St Paul can also speak of Christian men sharing, in a sense and in a measure, Christ's relation to God. It is God's purpose that these men should 'be conformed to the image of His Son, that he might be the first-born among many brethren' (Romans 8:29; cf 'the first-born from the dead', Colossians 1:18). In the Epistle to the Hebrews we find strong emphasis laid on the analogy between Christ's human experience and the experience of those men whom he saves. 'Both he that sanctifieth and they that are sanctified are all of one: for which cause he is not ashamed to call them brethren' (Hebrews 2:11; Weymouth translates 'have all one Father'). There also we find the purpose boldly expressed that all Christ's people should come to have the same kind of unity with Him, and through Him with the Father, as He has with the Father: 'That they may all be one; even as thou, Father, art in me, and I in thee, that they also may be in us: that the world may believe that thou didst send me. And the glory which thou hast given me I have given unto them; that they may be one, even as we are one; I in them, and thou in me, that they may be perfected into one; that the world may know that thou didst send me, and lovedst them, even as thou lovedst me' (John 17:21-23).

'He was made what we are,' wrote Irenaeus, 'that He might make us what He is Himself.'

If then Christ can be thus regarded as in some sense the prototype of the Christian life, may we not find a feeble analogue of the incarnate life in the experience of those who are His 'many brethren', and particularly in the central paradox of their experience: 'Not I, but the grace of God'? If this confession is true of the little broken fragments of good that are in our lives – if these must be described on the one hand as human achievements, and yet on the other hand, and in a deeper and prior sense, as *not* human achievements but things actually wrought by God – is it not the same *type* of paradox, taken at the absolute degree, that covers the whole ground of the life of Christ, of which we say that it was the life of a man and yet also, in a deeper and prior sense, the very life of God incarnate?

(*God was in Christ*, pp 125-129)

2 THE NEED FOR ATONEMENT
by Donald Baillie

AT this point of my argument the modern man will inevitably wish to ask: But why do you speak of *atonement* at all? Is not forgiveness enough? He might indeed point out – and other critics might agree with him from other points of view – that I seem in this matter to have cut the ground from under my feet by maintaining that God loves us equally through all our sins, that His love in no wise depends on our being worthy of it, but is eternally seeking us for our good, and that His forgiveness is free to all who will accept it. If that is indeed what Paul discovered in becoming a Christian, how could he afterwards work out a theology in terms of redemption, propitiation, reconciliation, through the blood of Christ? What room is there for an atoning sacrifice? Does not God's free forgiveness cover everything?

In reply to this I will ask another question: Is there no difference between a good natured indulgence and a costly reconciliation? There is an immense moral and spiritual difference between the two. And which of them are we to attribute to the love of God? Does the whole process of reconciliation cost him nothing? Is his forgiveness facile and cheap? And if it were, or if we accepted it as such, would it have the liberating power, to set us free for a new and better life?

When we speak of God's free love toward us, continuing unchanged through all our sin, and eternally ready to forgive us, there is always the danger that this should be taken to mean that God is willing to pass lightly over our sins because they do not matter much to Him; that it is all a matter of easy routine, about which we need not be greatly concerned and need not greatly wonder. The classical expression of this is in the oft-quoted words of the dying Heine: 'God will forgive me: that is his business.' (*Dieu me pardonnera: C'est son métier.' Souvenirs de la vie intime de Henri Heine,* by Princess della Rocca, Paris, 1881). This illustrates a real danger of misunderstanding the doctrine of divine forgiveness in a way which would make the whole idea morally unwholesome.

It is as if God were to be regarded as indulgent and good-natured, making as little as possible of our misdeeds, glossing over our delinquencies. Frederick Faber's hymn about the kind Shepherd and the frightened sheep has one verse which runs:

There is no place where earth's sorrows
Are more felt than up in heaven:
There is no place where earth's failings
Have such kindly judgment given.

After the simple truth of the first two lines the third and fourth lines always seem to me to make a very weak anti-climax, with the total effect of suggesting that God feels our sorrows much more deeply than our sins, and that His attitude to our sins can be described as mere 'kindly judgment'! Is God's love for sinners simply 'kindly judgment'? Nay, it is 'a consuming fire'. He cannot take our sins lightly or treat them with indulgence. 'The love that draws us nearer Thee is hot with wrath to them.' God must be inexorable towards our sins: not because He is just, but because He is loving; not in spite of His love, but because of His love; not because His love is limited but because it is unlimited, and because, as George Macdonald said, 'nothing is inexorable but love'.

We may, I think, find at least a faint analogy of this in the love of a true friend who receives a grave wrong but who generously forgives. If I play my friend false behind his back in a weak moment, basely betraying his confidence, and he discovers it, will he pass over it lightly, without any painful explanation and restoration? If he is a shallow soul, and not a very true friend, he may treat the matter in that light way, for the sake of comfortable relations, because he does not care very deeply for me. But he cannot do that if he is a good man and a true friend who loves me deeply. It is not that he will be slow to forgive me; but his forgiveness will not be a good-natured indulgence. It will come out of an inexorable fire of love which I shall shrink from facing. I shall be far more afraid to meet him and look him in the face than I should be if he were a shallow friend. So great a thing is his forgiveness.

But if these things are true, it is also true that in the whole great process of forgiveness it is my friend that has the hardest part to play. It is he that bears the brunt. He suffers more than I. Not because he is the person that has been wronged: nay, it is the shame of what I have done that weighs most on him. He bears my shame as if it were his own, because of his great love for me. He bears more of the agony than I, because he is a better man and loves more deeply. And it is out of all this noble anguish that his forgiveness comes. All that is what lies behind it.

How much more deeply all these things must be true of God, both in His judgment of our sins and in His 'atonement' for them! My human friend, whom I have wronged, knows that, after all, his is not the ultimate judge of my conduct. He will keep reminding himself that his judgment is fallible and apt to be one-sided, he will guard against being misled by his own *amour propre,* he knows the deceitfulness of his own heart so much better than he can know mine, and he will make all possible allowances. Even then he must be faithful with me if he loves me. But God loves me perfectly and knows me perfectly far better than I can know or love myself. If I have been disloyal to Him, as I have in all my misdeeds, I have been disloyal to the infinite Love which is the heart of the universe, which is the source and end of my existence, and the very meaning of the 'moral law' which I have broken. There can be nothing more inexorable than such a love. If I have betrayed it, that is the ultimate betrayal. That is what has to be wiped out, and such an 'atonement' must be the most difficult, the most supernatural, the costliest thing in the world.

But also – if we may follow the analogy farther – it is God that bears the cost. Our reconciliation is infinitely costly to Him. Not in the sense that it is difficult for Him to forgive us, as it would be difficult for a Shylock, who has to be induced not to insist upon his pound of flesh; not in the sense that He is inhibited from forgiving, by some hard necessity outside His own nature, so that there has to be an 'expiation' before God can act mercifully. It is His very nature to love and to forgive. He could do no other, and He has to wait for nothing but our response. Yet the forgiveness is not an easy amnesty, such as a good-natured tyrant might give with a stroke of his pen. It comes from the heart of a love that has borne our sins, and because the love is infinite, the passion is infinite too. 'Who suffers more than God?' asks Piers Plowman. There is an atonement, an expiation, in the heart of God Himself, and out of this comes the forgiveness of our sins.

It is from the sacrificial system of ancient Israel that we have inherited the whole terminology of atonement, expiation, propitiation, reconciliation; and it seems to me that after a long and puzzling story we find that system reaching in the Christianity of the New Testament a climax in which it is completely transformed into the idea of an atonement in which *God alone bears the cost.* The whole subject of sacrifice in ancient Israel is both complicated and controversial, but I must sketch the broad facts on which I base this statement.

The initial function of sin-offerings and guilt-offerings in Israel was the wiping out of ceremonial offences. In saying this, I do not imply anything as to the earliest meaning and purpose of sacrifices in Israel, or as to the point of time when they first came to be connected with the removal of sin and guilt; for both of these are controversial matters. But it may safely be said that when sacrifice did come to be regarded as a means of expiating offences, it was not the great and wilful moral offences, such as flagrant breaches of the Decalogue, that were in question, but the ritual offences which might be committed either unwittingly or through carelessness and without any very evil intent. These could be wiped out through the appropriate sacrifices. But for the remission of great and deliberate sins, dishonesty, violence, and the like, there was no such provision: God might indeed in some cases be induced to be merciful, but that would be something exceptional, on which nobody could count; and, in general, sinners must simply take their punishment. It is, of course, important to realize that this did not mean final and everlasting punishment in the next world, for the whole of that eschatological prospect of judgment was beyond the horizon. The punishment was in this world. For some great offences there was a civic punishment, inflicted according to the legal code. For others God would punish with misfortune, perhaps even to the third or fourth generation; sometimes with defeat in war and national calamity, if the offence were rather corporate than individual.

But in the great Prophetic movement which began in the eighth century BC two new notes appeared, and they are indeed among the glories of the prophetic message. First, the prophets began to proclaim, with immense conviction, that it is the moral offences (as we should call them) that really matter: injustice, dishonesty, bribery, perjury, oppression, violence, cruelty. These are the *real* sins, and so long as these go on, even if they keep on the safe side of the law, as they can so easily do under respectable disguises, God cares not at all for the most correct and profuse offerings and sacrifices: nay, He hates them and is disgusted with them, He will not accept them, or look with any favour on those who offer them. And the other new note was this: God will freely forgive even the greatest sins, if only the sinners will repent and turn from their evil ways. Nothing else is needed, no expiation, no offerings, for God has everything already. Sincere repentance is enough, and a real turning from sin to God; and then the sinner can count on God's mercy. 'Let the wicked forsake his way, and the unrighteous man his thoughts: and let him return unto the Lord, and he will have mercy upon him; and to our God, for he will abundantly pardon' (Isaiah 55:7).

Now a student of the history of Israel, finding these two new and epoch-making messages emerging in the prophetic movement, might expect to find the whole sacrificial system soon afterwards coming to an end, either by an official discontinuance or by a slow languishing into decay. But instead of this we find that in the Post-Exilic period the sacrificial system became more elaborate than ever, with more emphasis than ever on sin-and-guilt offerings, and not only in relation to ceremonial offences, but now with full and regular provision for the sacrificial expiation of *all* the sins of the people. Various explanations of this may be given. It may very well be that the great prophets themselves never meant that the sacrifices could be dispensed with altogether (this is a controversial point among specialists). Or it may be that there was always a gulf between the prophetic and the priestly tradition in this matter, though I think scholars now maintain that this has been greatly exaggerated. It may very well be also that as time went on the problem of sin and forgiveness and the need of expiation became more acute to the devout mind: because continuing national calamity seemed to speak of the divine displeasure; because with a deepening sense of the meaning of sin people felt that they were never able to make a perfect repentance and were slipping back into sin every day; and perhaps because there was also a deepening sense of the meaning of punishment as alienation from God, and an extension of its meaning beyond this world under the influence of the apocalyptic movement. All this might lead to a more earnest use of the sacrificial cultus, even by those who had best learnt the prophetic message of repentance and forgiveness. And so we come to the beginning of the Christian era.

Now when we turn from that long story to the Christianity of the New Testament, we find this extraordinary climax. On the one hand we find the Prophetic message of absolutely free forgiveness to the penitent sinner carried much farther than ever, with a definite extension that has been recognized even by Jewish scholars as surpassing anything ever taught by prophet or rabbi before. We find Jesus teaching that God not only freely forgives the sinner who turns to him in repentance, but goes out in quest of the sinner who has *not* repented, as a shepherd goes out into the wilderness to find the one lost sheep. On the other hand we also find the New Testament writers speaking of the long sacrificial tradition as having at last found its climax and fulfilment; but in such a way that its meaning is completely transformed, because now it is God Himself that makes the sacrifice. All the old terms are used, which we translate as sacrifice, offering, expiation, propitiation, atonement, reconciliation, and which meant so much to every Israelite who had a sense of sin. But now they have received a radically new interpretation, not only because they are applied figuratively to that Christian sacrifice which was not in the literal sense a sacrifice at all, but because it is ultimately God Himself that is regarded as bearing the brunt and paying the price. That is the remarkable witness, in many different forms, of the New Testament. Here is the 'reconciliation' which wipes out our trespasses, but we contribute nothing to the process: 'It is all of God'

(II Corinthians 5:18), who provides the means Himself. Just as Abraham 'did not spare his beloved son' but was ready to sacrifice him for God, so God 'did not spare his own Son, but gave him up [we might almost translate 'sacrificed him'] for us all' (Romans 8:32). Here is the sin-offering, but now the victim and the priest are one, and they are none other than the eternal Son of God, through whom he made the worlds, 'the effulgence of his glory and the impress of his substance' (Hebrews 1:1-3). Here also is the lamb sacrificed for the sins of men; but this Lamb is 'in the midst of the throne of God', this 'Lamb of God that taketh away the sin of the world' is none other than the eternal Word, the eternal God, by whom all things were made (Revelations 7:17; John 1:1,2,29).

Thus the two strains that we distinguished, from the age of the Prophets onwards, become one in their Christian climax: the strain that tells of God's readiness to pardon freely and abundantly, and that which persistently speaks of the need of costly atonement. God's forgiveness, as now understood in the New Testament, outruns all human attempts at expiation, because the expiation is made in the heart and life of God himself, the Divine Shepherd, who goes out into the wilderness in quest of the lost sheep. As I have already in this discussion quoted one simple popular hymn about the Divine Shepherd, I may be permitted to quote some imaginative lines from another:

'Although the road be rough and steep,
I go to the desert to find my sheep.'
But none of the ransomed ever knew
How deep were the waters crossed,
Nor how dark was the night that the Lord passed through
Ere he found the sheep that was lost.

That is the atonement for our sins that takes place in the very heart and life of God, because He is infinite love; and it is out of that costly atonement that forgiveness and release come to us.

(*God was in Christ*, pp 171-179)

3 THE THREE CROSSES
by Donald Baillie

And when they were come to the place which is called Calvary, there they crucified him, and the malefactors, one of the right hand, and the other on the left.

~ Luke 23:33 ~

THE subject before us concerns the execution of a condemned man which took place by crucifixion, under the Roman Empire, in the Province of Judaea, more than nineteen centuries ago during the procuratorship of one Pontius Pilate. It was an event that set men thinking more than anything else that has ever happened in the history of the world. Countless books have been written about it, countless pictures of it have been painted, and the image of that figure on the Cross stands at the heart of our religion. It is indeed an extraordinary symbol to stand at the heart of any religion. Why should it be there?

In one of the Irish plays of William Butler Yeats there is a vivid scene which perfectly expresses the objection which the human heart so often and so naturally makes against the religion of the Cross. The scene is in a country cottage in Ireland. The family are sitting together in the firelight of the kitchen, and on the wall there hangs a black wooden crucifix. There is a knock at the door, and when it is opened, in comes a little fairy girl, dressed in green, singing a merry song, the very personification of natural pagan happiness and the spirit of the green woods. Suddenly her eyes fall upon the crucifix, and she stops her singing and hides her face, and cries out: 'Take down that ugly black thing.'

There is the revolt of the religion of nature – I might say of our human nature – against the religion of the Cross. How well it expresses the question that we have all sometimes wanted to ask: Why should Christianity take that gaunt and tragic emblem and set it up at the heart of its message and in the centre of its world? Why must Christianity make so much of the death of Jesus, of his Cross?

I want to suggest that one sound way of answering that question may be found symbolically, but with a most natural and legitimate and even inevitable symbolism – in the words of our text. 'When they were come to the place which is called Calvary, there they crucified him, and the malefactors, one on the right hand and the other on the left.'

The Cross of Christ is not a solitary tragic cross, set up incongruously in the midst of a bright and happy world. It is a cross set between two other crosses, and we only understand its meaning when we look at the others too. Let us look then at the three crosses on Calvary.

(1) *The cross on the left hand* is tragic enough, sad and sordid enough. On it hangs a wretched criminal who is at odds with all the world, an outcast from society, and now dying an unspeakably painful and shameful death, with bitterness in his soul and at odds even with his fellow victims on that hill of Calvary.

That cross of the impenitent thief may well stand for all the sin and shame and suffering and tragedy of the world. That cross is the cross of all humanity. That man is everyman. And that cross explains why Jesus had to die, and why Christianity makes so much of his death.

We ask: Why does Christianity made so much of the Cross of Christ? In this fair and wonderful world, in which our hearts cry out for joy and feel that they were made for joy, why should the Christian religion introduce the Cross and make it dominate the landscape?

And the answer is: That is *not* what Christianity does or ever did. It was not Christianity that introduced the cross into the situation to cast its shadow. The cross was there already, and Christianity transfigured it. The cross was there already in ten thousand tragedies of human life. Quite literally, as I do not need to tell you, tens of thousands of men had died by crucifixion before Jesus did – tens of thousands of wretched thieves and murderers, rebels and runaway slaves. I wonder how many other crucifixions may have taken place in other spots all over the Roman Empire on that same spring morning on which Jesus was crucified. Even on that same spot, outside the gate of Jerusalem, there were two others.

Every schoolboy knew what it was to see the gaunt form of a cross standing out against the sky beside some highway, and to shudder as he passed. And that sums up all the sin and shame and pain of this fallen world. That was the situation into which Christianity came. That was the world with which it had to deal and which it had to save. And that is still the world we live in, as you very well know. You know very well too that it is not as though you and I could wash our hands of it. That impenitent thief – how much worse was he than the respectable people who passed comfortably by?

Perhaps he was more sinned against than sinning. Society could not wash its hands of him. He was the hapless victim, but the whole of society around was involved in the tangle of sin and shame that made an end of him. And we know that we are all involved in the tangle of sin and shame that has so many victims on the Calvaries of our time and has turned the world into a Golgotha.

Sometimes we are blind to it, sometimes we shut our eyes to it, and we want a romantic religion without a cross. But sometimes (and I am sure this happens to a great many young men and women in this present age), sometimes among all the sunshine and beauty we get a sudden vision of the immense tragedy of the life of humanity, and of our own share in the sinful responsibility for it, as sudden vision of the tens of thousands of shameful crosses that are destroying the life of mankind and the life of our souls.

And then we can thank God that Christianity has something to say about it. We can thank God that this Christian religion which has come down to us is a religion that faced the facts and went down into the depths and endured the Cross before it rose up to proclaim the victory and the glory of its Gospel. For the dreadful cross of humanity is always there – the cross of the impenitent thief.

(2) *The second cross, the one in the middle, is the cross of Christ.* It looks just the same as the others, and the passer-by would see no difference, except for the extraordinary superscription, which he could hardly take to be more than an ironical jest: Jesus of Nazareth, the King of the Jews! And yet Christian art has not

gone astray when it has painted the central cross in such a perspective that it dwarfed the others and drew all eyes. For that Cross of Christ is indeed the central fact in the history of the world. It casts a new light on the other crosses. It has made the very word 'cross' into a new kind of word altogether.

In the ancient world it was a word of sordid shame, just like the word 'gallows' or 'gibbet' in the modern world. But it became a sacred word. St Paul could speak of glorying in the Cross of Christ, and we can sing of 'the wondrous Cross on which the Prince of Glory died'. How did that Cross make such a difference? And what made it wondrous?

It was the One who hung on it and the spirit that was in Him as He embraced it.

We have grown so accustomed to the story of that divine drama of redemption in the subsequent light of the Christian faith that we commonly miss the element of terrible ordeal in the path that led our Lord to the Cross. We sometimes think of the crucifixion as if it were part of a prearranged drama in which our Lord had to play a settled part with a clear knowledge of the divine plot of the drama and of the triumphant conclusion. But it was much harder that that. He had to walk by faith and not by sight; and so far as sight could go, the cross that He saw looming doubtfully in His path must have looked as dreadful and final as anything could be, the very climax of shame and failure and tragedy, for Himself and for the people whom He had tried to serve and to save. The thing looked so dreadful that almost up to the last Jesus hoped and prayed that it might not come. If ever faith and love were difficult for any man in any situation, they were difficult for Jesus then. But Jesus went on with nothing in His heart except faith towards God and love towards men. And they crucified Him.

I said that the crucifixion of Jesus set men thinking more than anything else that has ever happened in the history of the world. And when men looked back and pondered on it, what did they think? This is the extraordinary thing: that it made them think of the love of God; not just of the love of Jesus, but of the love of God.

Of course they were looking back in the light of their resurrection faith. But they were looking back, surely, at the way in which Jesus had faced and endured the Cross. That was a new way of facing and overcoming evil. And it must be God's way. God must be like that. But was that precisely what they said, that God must be like Jesus? Nay, they said much more – God was in Jesus.

When Christ trod the *via dolorosa*, when Christ suffered and died, 'God was in Christ, reconciling the world unto himself'. God was not sitting remote in heaven, watching and judging the world from afar. God was there. God was involved in it, loving men with a love that would not give them up or let them go, however they might sin against it. This was God's own sacrifice. The victim was the Son of God. This was God Himself, bearing the brunt of the sin of men. This was the eternal love of God, bearing the sin and suffering of the world.

That is what men by stages learnt to say about the death of Jesus, and it is all over the New Testament. 'God commendeth his own love toward us, in that, while we were yet sinners, Christ died for us.' 'God so loved the world that he gave his only-begotten Son.' 'Herein is love, not that we loved God, but that he loved us, and sent his Son to be the propitiation of our sins.' And that was why St Paul could say, 'God forbid that I should glory except in the cross of the Lord Jesus Christ.'

That is the cross that stands in the centre.

(3) *The third cross is the one on the right hand, the cross of the penitent thief.* You remember the story. The man acknowledges that he deserved crucifixion, and that Jesus did not. Then he cries to Jesus: 'Lord, remember me when thou comest into thy kingdom.' And Jesus replies: 'Verily I say unto thee, today shalt thou be with me in paradise.'

Now, I will not discuss, as an historical question, what exactly that conversation meant at the moment. That would take too long and would perhaps be too difficult. But there can be no doubt as to what it has come to signify in the whole context of the Christian message. It signifies something that the crucified Christ has done with the sin and suffering of men. It signifies the light which the Cross of Christ sheds on all the shameful crosses in the world – not the kind of light that explains, but the kind of light that redeems, calling men to repentance and forgiveness and a new beginning and a place in God's Kingdom of love and service. It signifies for all time what Christ has done with the sin and suffering of the world.

I spoke of how you and I sometimes have a sudden vision of that mass of sin and suffering, that perennial cross of humanity. When we have that sudden piercing vision, I believe our hearts sometimes tell us that we must give our lives to the noble crusade of liberating our fellows from evil and making the world a better place. But very soon our hearts fail us, because the evil is so immense; and we ask ourselves hopelessly whether our petty efforts can make any difference to the measureless mass of evil in this ruined world. Very soon also we ask ourselves what right we have to try to change the world for the better, we who are so deeply involved in its sin ourselves.

But what if God in Christ has borne and is bearing the mass of sin and suffering? What if God through the cross of Christ is calling us to repentance, and offering to forgive us our sins? What if God is calling us, unworthy as we are, into His kingdom, that we may be its children and its servants in the world, bearing our share of the cross of humanity in the power of the Cross of Christ?

Then everything becomes worth while again. Even our feeble endeavours to serve God among men become abundantly worth while: we know now that they will not be wasted, they cannot be lost, because they are caught up and purified and accepted and used in the invincible cause of God's everlasting kingdom.

That is how Christ in His death, Christ reigning from the tree, stretches out His hands, to bless us with the forgiveness of our sins, and to call us into the service of His kingdom. As St Athanasius said sixteen hundred years ago, in words of magnificent symbolism: 'It is only on a cross that a man dies with outstretched hands.'

(*Out of Nazareth*, pp 62-68)

4 JESUS AND THE WORLD RELIGIONS
by John Baillie

THERE is a final question that is likely to be lingering in our minds. Are we really able nowadays to make quite the same exclusive claims for the religious significance of the single figure of our Lord as were made for Him in the Christian preaching of the past? Within a few months of the Crucifixion we find St Peter (if the account in *Acts* is to be trusted) boldly declaring in Jerusalem that 'neither is there salvation in any other: for there is none other name under heaven given among men, whereby we must be saved'. And it would not be difficult to parallel this declaration by statements from every other New Testament writer and from the literature of every succeeding generation of the Church's life. Has something of this note been forced out of our modern preaching?

Well, there is no doubt at all that in at least one notable respect we who live in this modern time are differently situated towards such a claim from any of our Christian predecessors, and particularly perhaps from our predecessors of the Middle and Reformation Ages. By far the most important and far-reaching of the many momentous changes which have come over our religious thinking during the last hundred years is the new attitude which we have adopted towards those religious cults which do not own the name of Christ. During at least fifteen of the nineteen centuries of Christian history it was the almost universal opinion of Christendom that there was no least particle of saving faith to be found anywhere in the world outside the rigidly defined bounds of the Christian communion. In Islam, in Confucianism, in Hinduism there was indeed admitted to be present a certain amount of true knowledge concerning God and the soul; but it was claimed that such knowledge was reached only by the *lux naturae* and contained no particle of faith or of grace or of revelation or of anything else that could avail in the smallest degree for the salvation of the soul. 'Thy best prayers are but as blasphemy and sin' – so, with the utmost courtesy of manner, said the crusading Knight of the Leopard to the Saracen Saladin in Scott's *Talisman*. We are all now agreed that this was great nonsense. We are most cordially prepared to allow that along some part of the way up which God has led us to Himself through Jesus Christ, He has also led other races upwards to Himself through other names than Christ's; and we even find no difficulty of principle in admitting that in these other and more partial revelations there may be here and there some new gleam of light to which the windows of our Christian tradition should be very hospitably open. Moreover that wistful old enquiry as to how Socrates could be allowed into heaven has lost all its meaning for us. If we were writing a new Apocalypse or *Paradiso* today, we should give the wise man of Athens a place very near the Throne. And so it may be felt that in adopting this changed point of view we have lost something of that note of urgency which has always characterised the proclamation of the Christian missionary message.

Yet here, as in so many other places, the real solution of our difficulty lies in going back to the direct and simple thinking of the New Testament itself. When we do thus go back, there are two very important discoveries which we are at once likely to make .... The first is that the New Testament claim that 'neither is there salvation in any other' is not in its essence an *a priori* theological dogma, such as it too readily became in later centuries, but rather a declaration of personal experience. It is true that when speaking to purely Jewish audiences the apostles showed themselves ready enough to make appeal to the supposedly predictive element in Jewish prophecy in order to prove the divine right of the Christian faith, but nothing could be clearer than that their *essential* appeal was always rather to the results of that faith as actually experienced in their own case. The New Testament writers were not academic philosophers but hard-working missionaries. The problem before them was not the intellectual one of the relative proportions of truth that there were in Judaism, in Stoicism, in Emperor-worship, in Mithraism, in the Orphic rites and in the Eleusinian mysteries, as compared with Christianity; it was the practical problem whether any of these 'ways' could really loose a man from his sins and bring him lasting joy and peace of heart. And their common declaration is that, whatever philosophic minds may say about degrees of truth and the like, yet in *their* experience not one of the many religious alternatives that were at that time before the Mediterranean world could in practice be relied upon (if we may allow ourselves this phrase) for 'doing the trick', save only the faith of Jesus Christ. What St Paul wrote to the Greek city of Corinth was not, 'There is nothing worth knowing in your local religion or in Stoic philosophy or in Orphic mysticism'. What he wrote was, 'I determined not to know anything among you save Jesus Christ and him crucified' (I Corinthians 2:2). It was not a theorem, you see, but a plan of campaign. It was not a dogma, but a challenge. And is it not a challenge we can still make unashamedly, and a plan which, as good strategists of the Kingdom of God, we shall still be wise to follow? 'I asked an earnest Hindu one day,' writes Mr Stanley Jones, 'what he thought of Christ. He thoughtfully answered, "There is no one else who is seriously bidding for the heart of the world except Jesus Christ. There is no one else on the field".' (op cit, p 62). Now, quite frankly, who else is there?

At the same time there is abundant evidence that the men of the early centuries were by no means blind to the fact that there was a real, though sadly limited, measure of truth and of saving efficacy in the other religions that were then known to the Roman Empire – particularly, of course, Judaism (which from the beginning was put in a class by itself as having been a necessary preparation for the Christian revelation), but also in Platonism and in Stoicism. And our second discovery is as to the way in which they dealt with the problem that was thus created for their minds. What they did was to say that wherever in the world there had ever been any real knowledge of, and effective communion with, the Divine Father, it must have been because there was there manifesting itself, in however limited a way and measure, the very same Spirit and Presence of God as was at last made fully manifest in Jesus of Nazareth. I say here the 'Spirit' and 'Presence' of God. These are the words which nowadays we should most naturally use in such a context, and they were used also in the apostolic age. But in that age ... there were certain other terms available which came even more naturally to men's minds. One such term was the 'Logos' or 'Word' of God; another was the 'Christ' or 'Anointed' of God. And, as we saw, these various terms, though having very different backgrounds of meaning and suggestion, yet came at last to be applied in so equivalent a way that often the choice of one of them for a particular context seems to have been made quite at random.

The Christian life was said, without distinction, to be a life in the Spirit, a life in Christ, and a life in the 'Logos'; the indwelling Presence in the Christian soul was said, indifferently, to be the Spirit of Christ or the Word of Christ; and that which had been made manifest in the flesh of the Carpenter of Nazareth was said, by different writers and in different contexts, yet with substantially the same meaning, to be God's Spirit, his Christ or his Word. And so, when a Jew would come forward and point to the real revelation of God that had been made in Old Testament history, those early Christians would say, 'Ah, that is nothing else but Christ in the Old Testament!' – choosing here the Jewish word 'Christ', because it was to Jews they were speaking. And when a Greek would come forward and make similar mention of Socrates and Plato and Zeno, the Christians would say, 'Ah, that was the same "Logos" who was perfectly manifest in the Carpenter of Nazareth making Himself imperfectly manifest in these other before the time was ripe!' – choosing here by preference the Greek word 'Logos', because they were speaking to Greeks. So it was claimed that in a large sense even Moses and David and Jeremiah, nay, even Socrates and Plato and Zeno, though living long before Jesus, were nevertheless to be reckoned as Christians, because something of that same Presence of God that was in Him had manifested itself also through them. After the intolerant exclusivism of much later history it is often surprising, and it is also refreshing, to find how large-minded were the earliest Church Fathers in this regard. 'Those who lived in company with the Logos,' wrote Justin Martyr in his second-century Apology, 'were Christians, even if they were accounted atheists. And such among the Greeks were Socrates and Heraclitus' (Apology, 1, 46).

* * *

Surely it is true that in the Old Testament and in Socrates, and in Gautama Buddha and Confucius too, we can find *something* of the same Spirit and Presence as was in our Lord Jesus Christ. Surely we ought to look upon our Christianity, not as excluding, but rather as including, the light that there is in other streams of religious tradition. Surely the only properly inclusive definition of Christianity is that it is the religion of all those who love God with heart and soul and strength and mind, and their neighbours as themselves. That, at all events, was the only definition of it that was ever offered by our Lord Himself.

There is indeed one important respect in which our spiritual horizon has immensely widened since these early days. The first Christians worked out their doctrine of the incarnation of the Word of God within a framework of pre-Copernican cosmology which made this tiny planet of ours the one and only centre of God's universe. It had never even remotely occurred to them that there could be other worlds inhabited by spiritual beings just as important as ourselves. We still do not *know* that there are such other inhabited worlds, but we are at least bound to leave fullest room in our minds for the probability. So we find one of our modern poetesses saying:

> *But in the eternities,*
> *Doubtless we shall compare together, hear*
> *A million alien Gospels, in what guise*
> *He trod the Pleiades, the Lyre, the Bear.*

> *O, be prepared, my soul!*
> *To read the inconceivable, to scan*
> *The million forms of God the stars unroll*
> *When, in our turn, we show to them a Man.*

~ Alice Meynell, 'Christ in the Universe' ~

And another we find saying:

> *For God has other Words for other worlds,*
> *But for this world the Word of God is Christ.*

~ Harriet Hamilton King, 'The Disciples' ~

Yet surely we can apply to these wider reaches of the divine self-impartation the same principle that the early Christians applied to such narrower reaches of it as were alone within their powers of conception. Surely we must believe that the Spirit or Word of God as it manifests itself in Mars or in some solar system or

Far in that faint sidereal interval
Between the Lyre and Swan.

~ J W Mackail, 'On the Death of Arnold Toynbee' ~

is essentially the same Spirit or Word whose glory we beheld in him who dwelt among ourselves, full of grace and truth. If God is truly One, then His Word must, as Plato and St John believed, be 'only-begotten' and eternally the same. And so, in that same sense in which our Fathers spoke of Christ being in the Old Testament and of Socrates companying with the Logos, we of to-day must think of the most distant fields of inhabited space as not lying beyond the redemptive reach of that selfsame love of God which was in Jesus Christ our Lord.

(*The Place of Jesus Christ in Modern Christianity*, pp 202-212)

(D) *The Holy Spirit*

1 THE DAY OF PENTECOST
by Donald Baillie

And it shall come to pass afterward, that I will pour out my spirit upon all flesh; and your sons and your daughters shall prophesy, your old men shall dream dreams, your young men shall see visions.

~ Joel 2:28 ~

This is that which was spoken by the prophet Joel; And it shall come to pass in the last days, saith God, I will pour out of my Spirit upon all flesh; and your sons and your daughters shall prophesy, and your young men shall see visions, and your old men shall dream dreams.

~ Acts 2:16,17 ~

'YOUR sons and your daughters shall prophesy, shall be prophets.'
What does that mean? What were those prophets whom we meet
so frequently in the Bible? What was a prophet? Not simply a man
who had a mysterious power of predicting future events, not a kind
of fortune-teller or crystal-gazer; but something much better. In
the highest sense of the word, a prophet was a man who could tell
the people about God's purposes, at first hand, because he knew
God for himself and could hear God's voice. In ancient Israel the
common run of people did not expect to be able for themselves to
enter into those mysteries. They took their religion with the
crowd, at second hand. What else could they do? They were
content to believe what they were taught, and do as they were told
– carry out their religious duties as decent members of the community. That was enough for most people. But sometimes – once
or twice in a generation – there would appear a man who was
different from the rest, a man who was obviously meant to be a
spokesman of God. Somehow the Spirit of God was upon him, he
could know God for himself, and enter into some of God's secrets,
and tell other people about God's mind and will. But of course
that could only be one man in a thousand, nay perhaps one in a
hundred thousand, one in a generation, a man apart, a friend of
God, a prophet.

And now, against that background, I wish to set before you
three very remarkable scenes from different parts of the Bible.

(1) The first is away back in the early days when the Israelites
were wandering through the wilderness under the *leadership of
Moses*. One day (so the story goes) Moses their leader stood and
said that he wished everybody could have God's Spirit and be a
prophet. He said it impulsively, in a generous moment, to show
that he wasn't selfish or jealous in these matters. He was a great
prophet himself, and one day when two other men began to set up
as independent prophets, outside his authority, his friends told
him, and expected him to put a stop to it. But he was too noble
for that; and he cried out, with a fine touch of imagination:
'Are you jealous for my sake? I wish to God that all God's people
were prophets, and that he would put his spirit on every one of
them.' Splendid generosity! But of course it was not intended as

a practical proposition – that the common run of people, the rank and file of humanity, should blossom out like that, and be able to talk about God for themselves. Yet was it not a remarkable utterance?

(2) My second scene is still more remarkable. A thousand years later another great man stood up and said that the thing would one day come true. He may not have been actually thinking of Moses' words, but that was the substance of it. It was *the man called Joel.* And he was convinced of it.

Now it is usually a dangerous thing to make sweeping statements about the future and the changes which the future will bring in human affairs. Such predictions often turn out quite wrong, for, as Chesterton says, history is very fond of playing the game of 'cheat-the-prophet'. But this man Joel was absolutely sure the thing was going to happen – that the time would come when all sorts of ordinary people would know God for themselves and have His Spirit. He was convinced that God had told him, and he put the words in God's mouth. 'It shall come to pass afterward, that I will pour out my spirit upon all flesh (*i.e.*, on all kinds of people); and your sons and your daughters shall be prophets, your old men shall dream dreams, your young men shall see visions; and even upon the servants and upon the handmaids in those days will I pour out my spirit.' What an extraordinary thing to say! How risky it must have sounded! To talk of ordinary people, young fellows and young girls, labouring folk and all sorts, having God's Spirit just as truly as the prophets, having heavenly visions and being able to talk about God for themselves! Joel did not say when he expected it to happen, or how long it would be, but he did say that it would come. And how remarkable! How unlikely!

(3) But here is the third scene, still more remarkable and unlikely. Four hundred years later another great man stood up and said that the thing had now actually just come true. It was *Simon Peter, on the Day of Pentecost,* as recorded in our text. And he said it because of things his own eyes were seeing, and everybody around him was also seeing, that summer day. It was in that same historic city of Jerusalem, where Joel had been a prophet. But now most people would have told you that Jerusalem's great days were past,

and it was a day of small things, spiritually. Most people would have told you that nowadays there were no great prophets, and that religion was at a pretty low ebb. But that summer day wonderful things were seen in Jerusalem: a host of people met together in religious fellowship, all sorts and conditions of men and women, but most of them very ordinary-looking, like the weather-beaten fisherman Simon Peter himself. And there they all were, eager and joyful, united in a new and wonderful fellowship, with a new light on their faces, because a new and supernatural thing had come into their lives. Moreover it was not a mere passing excitement. Some of the onlookers said it was, and shrugged their shoulders. But Peter knew better, and he spoke out. This was the work of God. What had happened to these people was that GOD had come into their lives as a great reality, and given life a new meaning and purpose. Hitherto they had taken their religion in a second-hand conventional way, as a venerable custom. But now it is different. Now they have a faith of their own, and it has brought them a new fellowship and a new courage, and they are prepared to go anywhere, in spite of danger, and testify to what they believe. God has come into their lives. And so Peter stood up and said: 'It had come true at last. This is what was predicted by the prophet Joel: It shall come to pass, saith God, that I will pour out of my Spirit upon all flesh; and your sons and your daughters shall be prophets, and your young men shall see visions, and your old men shall dream dreams. And even on my servants and handmaidens I will pour out in those days of my Spirit.' The wonderful thing had actually happened. The knowledge of God had become a thing for everybody.

What had happened to bring it about? Is it possible to give any answer to that question? Was there anything special, to which we can point? Yes, of course there was. There was – Jesus Christ. Jesus of Nazareth had lived among men in Palestine; and wherever He went, with His words and works, His faith and love, His sense of the presence of God – wherever he went, God became real, and ordinary people could understand Him. Ordinary people, who had never expected to be able to understand the mysterious things the prophets talked of – now they could, as they listened to Jesus.

That did not go on for ever, for presently Jesus got into trouble with the authorities, and was condemned and crucified. But very soon afterwards His people discovered that that did not make an end of it. He was not dead, He was alive, and now He was present in a more wonderful way even than when He was with them in the flesh. This was something new in mankind's knowledge of God, which had been supposed to be confined to the prophets and a few exceptional men, now coming into the hearts of all sorts of people, if only they would understand it and receive Him. That was the difference Christ had made, and that people realized on the Day of Pentecost, and that made Peter say that the old forecast of Joel had at last come true.

Now that is a very old story. Can we translate it into the language and the interests of our own modern world? Let us try, with the aid of a little imagination.

(1) You take your seat in a railway compartment. In the opposite corner sits a labouring man, reading his newspaper. You look at him and try to picture the life he leads. A rough bare life, you think; hard work all day, a quiet pipe in the evening, a football match to watch on a Saturday afternoon; and if he is a particularly decent man, he goes to church once in a while on a Sunday morning. So you sum up his life. Is that all? I wonder. When the man puts down his paper and leans back and shuts his eyes, what is he thinking of? Perhaps he is thinking of GOD. Perhaps he is bringing the light of his faith in God to bear upon the great issues he has been reading about in his newspaper – labour troubles, party politics, war and peace among the nations. Perhaps he is connecting all these things with the God he believes in. Why not? He is a working man. So was Jesus. And you don't know what depths of Christian faith there may be in the heart and life of that ordinary man.

(2) Or you go into a shop in the city. A girl at the counter serves you. What does she care for, except to get on as well as she can in her own line, and meanwhile get as much fun as she can out of her wages when working hours are over, a round of rather selfish and empty pleasures filling up her evenings and week-ends? And that is all. Is it? It may be. But it may be also that that girl has visions and dreams that would go straight to the heart of Jesus Christ

Himself. It may be that behind the scenes of what seems a very commonplace existence there is a brave unselfish life of burden-bearing for other people, sustained perhaps by the fellowship of the Church of Christ, and by a living faith in God.

You can imagine any number of cases. I think perhaps it would be best of all if we could have a glimpse of a Christian congregation at worship in one of the younger churches in Africa or India or China: a mixed company of men and women and children of different races, different colours, different castes and classes, different languages and degrees of education, and indeed every conceivable difference on the natural plane; and yet meeting together on a deeper level, with one heart and one soul, worshipping God in a supernatural unity, as one family of his; because they all have one thing in common – they have God, they have Christ, they have the communion of the Holy Spirit.

All these things are happening in the world, in those ways that I have been picturing and in countless other ways that you can picture for yourselves. And it is just what Joel said would happen, and what Peter said had begun to happen, coming true again in new ways in the twentieth century. 'I will pour out of my Spirit upon all flesh; and your sons and your daughters shall be as prophets, and your young men shall see visions, and your old men shall dream dreams; and even on my servants and on my hand-maids I will pour out in those day of my Spirit.'

In closing, let me ask two questions.

(1) Is all that as true of our generation as it has been of some past generations in Scotland? Is it happening as much as it used to happen – old men dreaming noble dreams of God's Kingdom, young men and women seeing heavenly visions of what God has done in Christ, and being captivated as his disciples? Is it happening as much today? I hope it is. I am sure it *is* happening. It is happening in quite new ways in Africa and India and China. But it is happening also in Scotland; in different ways, perhaps, from the ways of our forefathers, and expressed in different language (for one generation is not like another); but I am sure it is happening just as truly, because God is for everybody, Christ is for everybody, in every age.

(2) My second question is: What about ourselves? What about our own congregation? Have we in our midst the fellowship of the Holy Spirit, uniting us on the deepest level, because God has spoken to each one of us in Christ? What would the life of the Church of Christ, what would the life of this country of Scotland, have been through all the centuries without that kind of thing happening quietly and deeply among all sorts of people, from cottage to castle up and down the land? Friends, let us not miss it in our day and generation. The one aim and end of all we have inherited, all we have been taught, in our Christian homes and in the Church of Christ, is that we should, each one, and all in fellowship, come to have Jesus Christ as our own Lord and Master, the eternal God as our Father and our Friend, in the communion of the Holy Spirit.

(To Whom shall We go?, pp 31-37)

2 THE COMMUNITY OF THE HOLY SPIRIT
by Donald Baillie

And all that believed were together, and had all things in common; and they sold their possessions and goods, and distributed them to all, as any man had need. And day by day, continuing stedfastly in the temple, and breaking bread at home, they took their food with gladness and singleness of heart, praising God, and having favour with all the people. And the Lord added to them day by day those who were being saved.

~ Acts 2:44-47 ~

Is Christianity an individual Gospel or a social Gospel? Is it a matter of 'my soul and God', or is it concerned with the social and political order? Wherever I go just now I find that question being asked, and indeed hotly debated, with two opposite answers given. On the one hand I am told that a Christian's primary concern is with the salvation of his own soul in preparation for the world to come, and that the Church ought not to be directly interested in social or economic reform, because the real evil is the moral and spiritual evil in men's hearts, and it can only be dealt with by individual conversion. So true Christianity is an individual Gospel. Well, that sounds pretty deep. But then, on the other hand, I am told that true Christianity is a social Gospel, with a programme for the transformation of human society and a passion to make this world a better place for all sorts and conditions of men. Therefore, the Christian Church can't possibly stand aside from the social evils and problems of the age. It dare not keep silent about them, its message must be vitally concerned with them. And as for the individual, if he is more interested in saving his own soul than in securing social justice and opportunity for his less fortunate fellows, his religion is a religion of selfish escape, whereas true Christianity is a social Gospel.

These are the two sides of it, and they are constantly put up against each other in these days. On the one hand: 'What's the good of a social Gospel if our individual souls have not been saved?' And on the other hand: 'What's the good of an evangelical Christianity that doesn't deal with social evils?' Well, which of these is right? Is true Christianity an individual or a social Gospel? Does it speak to us of an individual salvation, or of a new social order?

Surely the right answer is 'Both'. And both together. They can't be separated, or they both go bad. I want to try to show that, with the aid of this story which all the Christian world is pondering on this Whitsunday – the story of Pentecost.

If you had been present as a sympathetic stranger in the city of Jerusalem on that Day of Pentecost, you would have been struck by two things. First, you would have been struck by the way in which all sorts of ordinary people had all at once come to have a personal religion of their own. In the ancient world, religion was much more a public matter than a personal matter, and the rank and file of humanity was hardly expected to have a personal knowledge of God. They were expected to take their religion on trust, at second hand, as decent citizens. Of course there were outstanding people, choice spirits, on whom God poured out his Spirit, and they became seers or prophets; they were very exceptional. They knew God directly. But now, you would have said on the Day of Pentecost, that seems to be happening to all sorts of people. They are coming to know God for themselves. Well, that is just what was happening. That was just what you'd have heard Simon Peter say in his speech. He said: 'This is what was predicted by the prophet Joel – It shall come to pass in those days, saith the Lord, that I will pour out of my spirit upon all flesh; and your sons and your daughters shall be like prophets, and your young men shall see visions, and your old men shall dream dreams; and even on my servants and handmaidens I will pour out of my spirit.' The fact is: the Gospel of Jesus had made religion a far more personal thing, for the ordinary individual, than it had ever been before, and it was on the Day of Pentecost that this came home to them. You'd have seen it quite plainly.

But if you had been there, you would also have been struck by another thing (here is the paradox). You would have noticed that religion had also, all at once, become a more deeply social thing than it had ever been before. Quite plainly, this was not any lone-wolf kind of religion. There was nothing solitary, or introverted, or cloistered, or escapist, about it. It was extraordinarily communal. These people – all sorts and conditions of men and women – seemed to have become a new community, with one heart and soul, with a new and wonderful comradeship that the world had never seen before. Quite true. The like of it had never been seen. And it was not mere emotion and sentiment. It was practical, and sacrificial. These people would do anything for each other – they even forgot all about the rights of private property, and made a little experiment in voluntary communism in Jerusalem. There sprang up a new kind of care for the poor, and presently a new attitude to slaves. They had a new sense of loyal responsibility for all their fellow-creatures, and they started to spread the good thing that had made them into a community. Of course they didn't embark upon a programme of social reform. They didn't even try to banish slavery. How could they? They had no political power in the great Roman Empire; most of them had no vote; they had none of the opportunities of modern democracy – that was far beyond the horizon. But the spirit was there – a spirit of community with all mankind – a new community without distinctions of class or race, in which every man was a child of God, a slave just as much as his master. *That was Christianity.*

Yes, and that is still true Christianity. And now that we do live in an age of democracy, where we all have voting power, and must all share responsibility for the dreadful evils of our social system, the Christianity that did not care about social reform would not be genuine Christianity at all.

There is an old Indian Buddhist story, which I believe has often been told in Christian pulpits, about a wise king who undertook to teach a young man the secret of spiritual freedom. This was how he did it. The young man was to be given a jar filled with oil to the very brim, and he was to carry it through the street of the town, where a fair was going on, without spilling a drop. An executioner, with drawn sword, was ordered to walk behind him, and upon the first drop of oil being spilt, was to strike off the young man's head. The young fellow agreed, did what he was told, and carried the jar safely back to the king without having lost a drop. The king asked him: 'As you walked through the town, whom and what did you see?' 'Sir,' said the young man, 'I kept my eyes fixed on the vessel of oil, and saw and heard nothing else.' And then the king told him that such was the secret of spiritual freedom: to be so intent on keeping one's own soul that one was blind to the affairs of one's fellows.

It is a good story. But that is a Buddhist parable for spiritual freedom. And now, for contrast, take the Christian picture. It comes just after the story of Pentecost, and the people of whom it speaks are the people who had had that deep personal experience of the Holy Spirit of God, searching out the depths of their individual souls. But this is how it showed to the world: 'And all those who believed had all things in common, and they sold their possessions and goods, and distributed them to all, as anybody had need. And day by day, continuing steadfastly in the temple, with one accord, and breaking bread in private houses, they took their food with gladness and singleness of heart, praising God, and having favour with all the people. And the Lord added to them daily such as were being saved.'

'Being saved': What does that mean? It does not mean a passport for a place called heaven. It means being transformed into the sort of person that can't bear to see his fellow-creatures missing the true opportunities of life, or living in conditions he wouldn't live in himself. But doesn't salvation mean being set free from my sins? Yes, and sin is equal to self-centredness, and my supreme sin is that I don't care enough about the welfare and the woes of my fellows, both spiritual and material. Perhaps my greatest sin is that when there were three millions of unemployed folk in this country, and hundreds of thousands of youths being ruined by it in body and soul, I didn't care anything like enough about it. And if we don't care enough yet, and if, when that kind of problem comes again, we haven't cared enough to find a way out – we Christians – that will indeed be the day of judgment for the Church of Christ, showing that it has substituted self-centred sentimentalism for the Pentecostal spirit of community.

Now let me not be misunderstood. I do not for one moment mean that the Christian Church or pulpit should preach political programmes. But it ought to denounce social evils, and it ought to stab awake the consciences of its members about the great sin of their social callousness. Again: I do not suggest that everyone who shouts slogans of social reform is near the Kingdom of God or the Gospel of Christ. It is quite easy to make that kind of thing an escape from God and from Christ. It is dreadfully easy, especially if we have some discontents of our own, to shout slogans about a new social order, and even to get fussy and busy about social reform, without really caring a scrap about our fellows – without one drop in our hearts of the milk of human kindness, nor to mention Christian love. That kind of thing may be just a feverish escape from God and our own souls. That's no use. But what I do say is: that when we do hear God's voice through Jesus Christ, it calls us out of ourselves into community with God and man. And then individual Gospel and social Gospel become all one – we can't separate them, without killing both, and running away from God.

So I want to close with one word of appeal, not so much to the people of my generation, but to you young men and women, whose life lies before you. My friend – whoever you are – I don't

need to tell you that there is something dreadfully wrong with the
world you live in. Also I don't need to tell you that there is something wrong with yourself. And how can you care about getting
the world put right for other folk until you have got yourself
put right? And yet how can you get yourself put right except by
coming to care more for other folk – because what is wrong with
you is self-centredness?

That seems a queer tangle. Well, the Gospel of Christ has everything to do with that tangle. God was incarnate in Jesus Christ,
and He created in the world a new community – the fellowship of
the Holy Spirit – to draw us out of ourselves into community with
God and man, for our own salvation and the salvation of the
world.

And if you, my friend, feel your heart pierced, in this your day
and generation, by the woes of your fellows, that is perhaps the
beginning of God's work in your heart, saving you from yourself,
drawing you out of yourself, into a life worth living, where you
will be lifted above your own temptations and defeats by the
enthusiasm of the service of God and man, in the Community of
the Holy Spirit.

If God is beginning that work in you – let Him have his way.

(*To Whom shall We go?*, pp 66-72)

(E) *The Church*

1 A New Humanity
by Donald Baillie

IF we might make bold to view this matter in another 'myth' or
divine emblem, I would tell a tale of God calling His human children
to form a great circle for the playing of his game. In that circle we
ought all to be standing, linked together with lovingly joined
hands, facing towards the Light in the centre, which is God ('the
Love that moves the sun and the other stars'); seeing our fellow
creatures all round the circle in the light of that central Love,

which shines on them and beautifies their faces; and joining with them in the dance of God's great game, the rhythm of love universal. But instead of that, we have, each one, turned our backs upon God and the circle of our fellows, and faced the other way, so that we can see neither the Light at the centre nor the faces on the circumference. And indeed in that position it is difficult even to join hands with our fellows! Therefore instead of playing God's game we play, each one, our own selfish little game, like the perverse children Jesus saw in the market-place, who would not join in the dance with their companions. Each one of us wishes to be the centre, and there is blind confusion, and not even any true *knowledge* of God or of our neighbours. That is what is wrong with mankind. Of course a man is not really happy in that attitude and situation, since he was created for community with God and man. Moreover, the light of God is still shining from the true centre upon his back, though not on his face. It throws his own shadow on the ground in front of him, and the shadow is contorted into grotesque shapes with every movement that he makes, until his whole world looks queer and unfriendly (it is indeed a fallen world, a ruined world). He knows, dimly or clearly, that all is not well. Perhaps he tries to *make* himself happy by pursuing his dance more furiously, but then his shadow dances still more mockingly, and things are worse than ever. For, as moralists have so often said, the quest of happiness defeats itself. Perhaps he even tries to mend matters by making himself good. But again he does not succeed. For, though this is not so obvious to moralists, the quest of goodness also defeats itself. The whole procedure of trying to improve our own characters keeps us thinking about ourselves. It is selfcentred, and self-centredness is the very thing from which we need to be saved, because it is the essence of sin. That method fails, and failure brings discouragement and moral paralysis. Or if we ever begin to succeed in improving ourselves, or even to think we are succeeding, then we congratulate ourselves secretly on our achievement, which is the very worst kind of self-centredness – self-righteousness and pride. So instead of becoming saints, we become 'Pharisees'. (I have left our 'myth' behind: it has served its purpose, and I must not ride it to death.)

If that is what is wrong with the world, it is difficult to see how it could be put right. It seems impossible to change ourselves from being interested mainly in ourselves to being concerned with God and our fellows, because the more we try, the more are we concentrating on ourselves. How could we save ourselves *from* ourselves? We need to be drawn *out of* ourselves into the life of unselfish community: and how could we possibly do that?

But God has never given mankind up. He has always had His purpose. And (so far as we can venture to describe the divine plan in human history) His method of saving mankind has been like this. Thousands of years ago He started a new community, a little one at first, in order that it might be the nucleus of a new mankind. It was the people of Israel, the 'chosen People'. It consisted of ordinary men and women, who were sinners like the rest of mankind. But God drew them into a kind of compact, a 'Covenant', as they called it; and so they became in a special sense God's community, or (as they sometimes called it when they spoke Greek) the *Ecclesia* of God (as in the Septuagint). It was not that He was going to treat them as pampered favourites: far from it! He chose them, not for their own selfish sakes, but (though they did not usually realize it) for his great purpose of saving mankind. This would make high demands upon them (God would have to be stricter with them than with any other people) (Amos 3:1,2) but it would be worth while. For they would find their own salvation in being used for the salvation of mankind. Thus they would be a redeemed and redeeming community, through which all the world would be drawn back out of its disintegration into the life of community with God and man, and so the nucleus would grow into a new mankind.

But Israel would not learn the lesson or rise to the occasion. Israel took its vocation in a selfish sense, and would not go far enough with the great purpose of God. Only a few men here and there, only a 'faithful remnant', proved to be willing and ready. Israel as a whole would not understand, and missed the opportunity of being the nucleus of a universal community of God.

And then God, whose 'counsel standeth for ever', who would not give mankind up; created a new nucleus for humanity by becoming incarnate Himself in a man of that race of Israel that had been so disappointing. This man Jesus, living in the midst of disintegrated sinful humanity, and subject to all its temptations, lived the kind of life that God meant all men to live. He was content to lose Himself entirely in the life of God and the life of his fellow-men, living without reserve the life of community, which is the very life of God Himself, though there was no community that would live it with Him, or even tolerate His living of it. He gathered around Him a dozen plain men, to make a beginning with them, though they hardly understood Him at all. They could not believe that 'the man who preserves his life will lose it', though they saw that their Master was not 'preserving' his life. He claimed nothing for Himself, not even life; and eventually His venture did cost Him His life. The people could not understand it, they got Him condemned to death. Even His chosen disciples deserted Him. He Himself was now all that was left of the 'faithful remnant' of the People of God, and He died on a cross, forsaken and alone.

But God had not given mankind up, and His purpose was not defeated.

A few weeks later, in that same city of Jerusalem where Jesus was condemned and crucified, we can see the most marvellous community that the world has ever known. It consists of those disciples of Jesus, now reunited, and a host of others with them, living in the warmest and closest fellowship, and growing in numbers every day and hour: the Church of Christ. Where has it sprung from? What has happened in that tragic and apostate city? How have those disciples been drawn out of themselves into this marvellous new fellowship, drawn out of the fallen pride of their dreadful failure, out of the inveterate and cowardly selfishness of their human nature, into the love of God and man? How had the impossible thing happened to them, or begun to happen? If we had asked them, they would have told us that their Master was not dead but alive, and even present with them. God had brought Him safely through death and raised Him up, and given Him back to them in an unseen way through what they called the Holy Spirit; and this had made them into a new community, with a wonderful solidarity which they called 'the fellowship of the Holy

Spirit' and which God was using to draw other people in. But they would have told us something even stranger: that it was not only their Master's resurrection or His living Spirit that was doing such marvellous things – His very crucifixion, which had so scandalized and scattered them, had a great deal to do with it, and was indeed at the heart of the secret. For now, looking back, they could see that this was actually the love of God dealing with the sins of men, offering them forgiveness and a new beginning if only they would come and accept it. That was what had broken down their self-centred pride (which is always the real trouble, separating us both from God and from each other) and made them willing to come back into fellowship, not as good and worthy men who had a right, but as sinners all alike in need of mercy. Others were drawn in, and the community grew; and they kept thinking and saying ever more and more stupendous things about the man Jesus and His crucifixion: that this was God's sacrifice of His own son for the salvation of men; that this was the eternal divine word becoming incarnate and suffering as the Lamb of God that bears the sin of the world. This was the love of God Himself, exposing itself to the consequences of human sin, coming all the way in quest of sinners. These things made even Pharisees content to call themselves sinners and as such to enter the new community. It was indeed a new kind of community: a society of sinners forgiven, with the cross as its badge, and every member confessing: 'Not I, but the grace of God.' That breaks down the barriers between man and man, and the members come to love each other because God first loved them and drew them out of themselves into the unity of 'one body'. That is the new People of God, the new Israel, the *Ecclesia,* the Body of Christ, the Church.

And this is the nucleus of a new humanity. It can never be content to remain a remnant, because its spirit is the spirit of divine love: not only towards it own members but towards all men. Its members will be interested not only in men's souls but in all that concerns their bodies too, all their material and social welfare, because God in His love came right into our material world. His Word was made flesh. It will transcend all barriers of class and race and nation, because from the standpoint of the

Community of the Cross there is no difference: all are sinners and all can be saved. This new and universal community was created by what God did in Jesus Christ, and is based on nothing else: and through it God draws other men into community, and so saves the world. This, we can now say, is what God was preparing the world for when He chose and called the People of Israel. They did not know it, but God knew it; and as St Paul said, this was God's great secret, the 'mystery' which had been laid up for countless ages but was now revealed: that 'Israel' would be transformed into a universal community, based not on Hebrew race but on faith in Jesus Christ, open to all men, the nucleus of a new mankind, the Israel of God. It is the Body of Christ. It shares in the sufferings, as it keeps the Festival, of the Broken Body. And it cannot be content until all men have been drawn into its fellowship, even if the perfect consummation must lie beyond the bounds of terrestrial history. It can never be content until mankind is truly 'one body' according to the eternal purpose of God – 'till we all attain unto the unity of the faith and of the knowledge of the Son of God, unto a full-grown man, unto the measure of the stature of the fullness of Christ: that we may be no longer children (refusing to play God's game because we want to play our own) … but maintaining the truth may by love grow up wholly unto him who is the Head, even Christ: from whom all the body, fitly framed and knit together through that which every joint supplieth, according to the working in due measure of each several part, maketh the increase of the body unto the building up of itself in love' (Ephesians 4:13-16).

Thus the Church of God's instrument of reconciliation through the ages. And to that end the perennial function of the Church is to proclaim, by Word and Sacrament and by its whole life, the message of what God has done in Jesus Christ. It is the Church, and it is only the Church, that can tell the story, the 'sacred history', because it is a confession and a testimony among men: TO WIT, THAT GOD WAS IN CHRIST, RECONCILING THE WORLD UNTO HIMSELF, NOT IMPUTING THEIR TRESPASSES UNTO THEM, AND HATH COMMITTED UNTO US THE WORD OF RECONCILIATION.

. (*God was in Christ*, pp 205-210)

2 SECULARISM AND THE EVANGELICAL TASK
by John Baillie

WHEN Chalmers spoke ... of the vital necessity of 'upholding a diffused Christianity throughout the land', he did not mean what is now commonly described by that phrase. What he hoped to uphold was a condition of things in which, though not all might personally and in saying faith be appropriating to themselves the inward blessings of the Gospel, yet all implicitly acknowledged the truth of the Christian creed, the duty of Christian worship and the authority of the Christian standards of conduct. What has happened between his day and ours is that the public standards of conduct have been more and more divorced from the creed and the worship. Diffused Christianity to-day means only the surviving influence of Christian moral ideals after the impulse of worship has failed and the belief grown dim and shadowy. It is in defence of this kind of diffused Christianity that our people are to-day fighting so valiantly. They are defending a certain type of civilisation, a certain way of living, and especially a certain way of living together. It is a way of living for whose introduction into the world Christianity has been mainly responsible. Sometimes this is recognised, and then men will say that it is Christian civilisation they are fighting for; sometimes it is not recognised, and then men will be content to ground themselves on 'the rights of man', on 'democratic principles' or on 'the interests of the proletariat' according to their several lights. But whether recognised or not, the historian knows it to be true, and in either case what we are confronted with is the development of what the biologists would call a 'fission' within the old unity of Western civilisation. There was a day when the men of goodwill were the men who went to church, while the men who stayed away from church were for the most part men of mischievous will. Having no part in the believing and worshipping life of the community, the latter were strangers also to its common ways of life. But now the world is full of men of goodwill whose high idealism and social-mindedness is such as often to put believing and worshipping Christians to shame, but who themselves neither worship nor believe. Many will find an extreme example of such fission in the recent break-up of the traditional Christian sentiment of Russia into a fervour of social-mindedness that definitely repudiated Christian belief and worship, and on the other hand the believing and worshipping piety of an Orthodox Church that was gravely lacking in social-mindedness; and if we read in the life and times of Voltaire we may see the same thing already happening in France two hundred years ago. Whatever we ourselves think about the situation in Russia, we must face the fact that it confronts large numbers of our people with the problem of a divided loyalty. Moreover, quite apart from Russia or any other foreign country, we have the compelling fact that in our own land of Scotland there is now a large fund of goodwill and charity and brotherly kindness which is outside the Church and yet sets an extraordinarily high standard of sacrificial living to those of us who are within.

That is the very crux and apex of the Church's problem to-day; and it is the crux of my personal problem that among my own neighbours and associates there should be many men who neither worship nor believe but whose lives are in many respects a continual judgment on my own. Nor is it as if these men were pagans, practising a pagan virtue such as might be associated with a pagan belief and worship. It is Christian virtues they are practising, while their spirituality, though so largely neutral, is (I must repeat) at least more Christian than it is anything else. And if you try to comfort me by saying that their virtues are nevertheless but splendid vices because they do not proceed from right beliefs, that only drives me to ask myself whether my own right beliefs are not then but splendid heresies, because they do not yield a better fruit.

This does not mean that I am not at the same time dominated by the feeling and knowledge that these neighbours of mine lack that which is the very deepest secret of human blessedness. Something is wanting even from the quality of their goodness, as compared with a goodness which it has elsewhere been my privilege to know. I am quite sure that only in genuinely Christian lives and in genuinely Christian homes is the rarest flower of virtue to be found. The most finely-tempered souls that have come within the circle of my own acquaintance have one and all been practising and professing Christians from whose daily and hourly reliance upon divine grace there has issued a sweetness and serenity and joy – I think above all a radiant joy – such as I have elsewhere missed. The hymn speaks truly:

> *Solid joys and lasting treasure*
> *None but Zion's children know.*

For it is not only that the quality of such unbelieving and unworshipping goodness lacks something very precious, but also that, as I have already said, there is always the haunting doubt of its lastingness, its ability to perpetuate itself from generation to generation in this disengaged form, its capacity to maintain itself intact against the powerful contrary forces that now advance against it so menacingly from the right and from the left. How much these good and charming people are missing, how much also they are *risking,* when they refuse the fellowship of the Church of Christ!

If this is the crux of the Church's problem, it is to this situation that the Church's present strategy must be directed. Because it is a new situation, it must be a new strategy. Many and far-reaching changes are to-day needed in what Chalmers called 'the outward business of the house of God', but at the same time changes in our evangelic approach – in the presentation to the minds of our contemporaries of the unchanging evangel of Christ. And the main question precisely concerns the kind of appeal we are to make to that large body of Scotland's manhood whose high qualities of character and ideals of service are such as often to rebuke us, yet who, though most of them have received Christian baptism and seek a Christian consecration of their marriage and Christian burial for their dead, take little or no further part in the Church's worship and find little meaning in its creed. It is sometimes said that we are now faced in our own homeland with a fundamentally missionary situation, and that our preaching to large masses of our people must be of the kind we address to pagan races in other lands; but that, I am persuaded, is only a half-truth. Scotland may indeed be threatened with a reversion to paganism, but it is not pagan yet, nor can I think that a wise strategy will address it as if it were. Our address must rather be such as to display the most understanding and sympathetic and imaginative adaptation to the particularity of the situation which we actually find to exist and the leading features of which I have tried to describe.

What our nation needs to-day is spiritual revival. Such revival cannot be engineered by ourselves but only granted us by God whose winds blow where he lists. We fervently pray that when our gallant youth return to their towns and villages, to their factories and farms, they may return also to a deeper sense of Christian community than that from which they went out; yet we cannot hope to foresee in just what way this prayer will be answered or from what quarter such a movement of the Spirit will chiefly proceed. But let our ears at least be open to the sound of it, let our minds be hospitable to receive it and our hands ready for the tasks it will entail, however different it may outwardly appear from the visitations of former days.

('Prospects of Spiritual Renewal',
Address to the General Assembly 1943, pp 17-22)

3   CHRISTIAN CIVILIZATION
by John Baillie

ONE can hardly imagine how the Church's history would read to-day if it had not been subjected to the constant criticism of the sects. Certainly the history of the Dark Ages would have made sorry reading if it had lacked the austere witness of monachism; while an even more important part has been played by the dissident movements from Montanism down to Methodism, as well as by various groups which, though not seceding from the national Churches, have fulfilled a like office within them. And in our own day we owe much to those prophetic voices which warn us that the Church, in seeking to maintain its alliance with a growing secularist community, is in danger of growing itself more secular-minded.

If it has always been difficult to be in the world without being also of it, the difficulty has never been greater than it is to-day. Never has the Christian doctrine of regeneration stood in more danger of neglect. Never have men more needed to be told that Christ prefers to have them cold than to have them lukewarm. Never have Christians more required to learn again, in groups however small, the true and original meaning of Christian togetherness in the communion of saints. Never has the Church had more need to be reminded that its first aspiration, no matter what kind of world it finds itself occupying, must be to become such a Church as its Lord desired to present to himself, 'not having spot, or wrinkle, or any such thing' (Ephesians 5:27).

Very great weight must therefore be given to the protesting movements of which I have spoken, and the Church is little likely to flourish if it fails to take up into itself a great part of the thought and feeling which they represent. Nevertheless I cannot think that they have the whole truth within their grasp. The question ultimately turns on the measure in which we believe the Church to have been justified in the principles governing its admissions to baptism in the various periods. And here I should lay the greatest possible stress on the distinction between what I have called the open Christian civilization of the modern period and the compulsive or conscriptive civilization that preceded it. It is only the former that any of us is likely to be found defending at this time of day. We are all firm believers in the principle of toleration which, though born of the indecisiveness of the wars of religion, and nourished in its youth by the success of the Protestant dissenting minorities in their struggle for independence, reached its maturity only in the admission of acknowledged unbelievers to the equal citizenship of the Western nations. None of us wishes to have the exercise of civil rights again associated with Church membership. None of us desires to return to an ecclesiastically dominated society. And however much we may long for a recovery of something of the unity that formerly pervaded all departments of life and thought, and a reconquest of what have been called the 'lost provinces' of our religion, we are equally concerned to retain for these a large part of the freedom they have gained and at least such a relative autonomy as was denied them by the compact medieval pattern of unity. Up to this point, then, I agree with Mr Middleton Murry when he writes in his latest book that 'Whether we call the Church-inspired and Church-governed civilization of the Middle Ages a Christian civilization is of minor importance compared with the necessity of realizing, quite clearly, that that civilization has completely perished. It is no use trying to cling to scattered spars from the wreckage of that civilization' (*Adam and Eve*, 1944, p 74).

But it has long seemed to me that the element of truth to which too little weight is given by the protesting movements is that contained in the Christian doctrine and practice of the baptism of families – a doctrine and practice which, very significantly, was a main target for the criticism of some of the more extreme of these movements, from Montanism to Anabaptism. The insight enshrined in this doctrine and practice is that the most likely way to bring men to an individual decision for Christ is to nurture them within a Christian community. This community is in the first place the family, and hence the controversy has always revolved round the baptism of infants born to Christian parents. But it is necessary that something of the same principle should be extended also to those larger social units in which, as the child grows to adolescence and manhood, he finds himself increasingly involved; and this is all the more necessary in a day like our own, when the family unfortunately counts for so much less in adolescent life than it used to do.

Just, therefore, as it is wrong to think meanly of the Christianity of children before they reach the age of personal decision and are confirmed in the faith, so I believe it wrong to hold as of no account the Christianity which pervades the life of a community before it is confirmed in the personal decision of every individual citizen. It is very evident, for instance, that Calvin's defence of paedobaptism and his championship of community religion were ultimately rooted in a single principle in his mind. While it was only to the children of baptized adults that he would administer baptism, this actually meant that he administered it to all children, since 'to be a citizen of Geneva it was necessary to make a profession of faith in Christ'. Calvin knew that many who made this profession were not truly regenerate, and that many of the homes into which children were born were therefore not truly Christian; and he taught that in these cases baptism was unaccompanied by the promised blessing; but he did not profess to know with anything like certainty which or how many these cases were, and he was accordingly not deterred from a practice which at least ensured that the children of Christian parents should be adopted in earliest infancy into the membership of the Church. It is, it seems to me, by a legitimate extension of the same principle that Mr T. S. Eliot defines a Christian society as a society of 'men whose Christianity is communal before being individual' (*The Idea of a Christian Society,* p 59).

(*What is Christian Civilization?*, pp 33-36)

4 CHRISTIANITY AND POLITICS
by John Baillie

.... NEVERTHELESS, when the full light of the Gospel is cast upon it, all earthly civilization, including that which has been most permeated by Christian influence, becomes subject to ultimate criticism as falling under the final judgment of God. A society which has a 'Christian tone' without being completely Christian in substance, though it may represent the best attainable in a world of sin, is clearly not a conception in which the mind can rest. It is what M. Maritain calls an *ambivalent* conception. Such an earthly city, he says, is no realization of the divine ideal, but only a kind of refraction of it. Yet because it is a refraction of the true light, and because no full realization is possible in a fallen world, Christian criticism must, as I have already argued, never be pushed to the extreme of disengagement from its problems. Least of all in our own time is it permissible for Christians to adopt such an attitude. The ills of our present social order are such that the Christian who refused to interest himself in the mending of them could at best salve his conscience by retiring into a monastery, and the Church by withdrawing 'into the catacombs' of a small-scale social order of its own making. That too would be an evasion of duty, but an evasion of a less offensive kind than that involved in complacently accepting the amenities, and availing ourselves of the privileges and amenities in a cruelly unjust way, so that others are necessarily debarred from much that we ourselves enjoy. Christians who to-day defend the Church's slowness to concern itself with social reform by standing fast on the distinction between 'religion and politics', or between 'religion and economics', too often find themselves in the same camp as those men of the world whose opposition to projected reforms proceeds only from the defence of their own vested interests in the existing order. Such a clean-cut discrimination of the religious sphere from the economic and political may have served a useful purpose in former orders of society; within Medievalism where pope and emperor represented parallel functions of a single, and withal a Christian, society; or even within the liberalism of Victorian Britain where a single general mind prevailed among the leaders of both Church and State, so that the discrimination in question hardly meant more than a natural division of labour. But as the society of the West has become less and less Christian, what was once only a division of labour has of necessity grown more and more into a conflict of principle.

Hardly more tenable, though not infrequently put forward, is the view that the Church's criticism of the social order must confine itself to a merely negative role. The Church, it is said, must expose the injustices of the existing order, and must vigorously protest against them, but is not called upon to point the way to better alternatives. This, however, is to condemn the Church to the most thankless of all tasks – to the task of attempting to destroy what it will not help rebuild, raising a carping voice where it stretches out no guiding hand. It would, no doubt, be an equally grave disaster, were the Church so to concern itself with the detail of political and economic arrangements as to become a party in the State or to align itself with a particular party programme; for party government is of the essence of the liberal order, and, while anything of that remains, the distinction between the spheres of religion and politics must retain a large measure of validity. Fortunately, however, those who so advise us are few. The imminent danger is not in that direction, but is rather the danger that, by allowing the political and economic order to take care of itself, the Church of Christ will tragically fall short of its duty of bringing the light of the Christian Gospel to bear upon every activity of the common life.

Nevertheless, as I have said, even the most Christianized of earthly civilizations is seen by Christian faith to fall under the ultimate judgment of God. For however strenuously we may oppose Ranke's use of the fact that every moment of temporal history is equidistant from eternity, and the consequent doctrine, represented in the words already quoted from Dr Dehn, that no one form of social or cultural order is nearer to the Kingdom of God than any other, it still remains true that even the nearest form is very far away. 'True justice does not exist,' wrote St Augustine, 'save in that republic whose founder and ruler is Christ – if we choose to call it a *respublica* on the ground that it is undeniably a *res populi.*' St Augustine was no doubt unduly pessimistic in his estimate of earthly possibilities, but the reason he proposes for his assertion that the Christian can never offer more than a qualified loyalty or attachment to any earthly civilization remains as valid as ever. It is that every earthly civilization is a civilization largely corrupted by sin, and that the only justice it knows is therefore the kind of justice which can exist in a society of men who remain largely unjust in their own individual desires. This insight is represented throughout almost the whole history of the Church by the distinction, already implicit in the thought of St Augustine's predecessors and remaining in general currency until long after the close of the Middle Ages, between what may best be called the absolute and the relative Law of Nature. The prior and simpler distinction between the various nations, and the Natural Law which was the foundation of them all as well as the criterion by which the justice of each must be appraised, had already been taken over by Christian from pagan thought, the natural Law being identified with the Divine Law of Nature was a law adapted to the conditions of a sinful world; and does not therefore represent either God's original or his ultimate design for human living, as represented respectively in the conceptions of a Primitive State before the Fall and of a final Kingdom of Heaven after the close of history. In that design there is no place for force or compulsion; for penal action or any kind of restraint; for distinctions of master and servant, or of rich and poor; for the holding or defending of private property; or for any such thing. It is a design for a way of life in which there is no wrongful self-interest needing to be curbed, and in which all may accordingly be left in the hands of spontaneous love ....

Yet the attempt to put this ultimate Christian ideal into practice in the life of the world, and even the attempt to put it perfectly into practice in the life of a monastic community, would lead only to anarchy and chaos, and to the disappearance even of that kind and degree of justice which can be achieved through the adoption of the relative ideal. It follows that the Christian's attitude to civilization must be a double one. He must strive to bring it as near to the Christian ideal of life in community as is possible in a world of sinful men, but he must never give it his absolute approval or unconditional loyalty; he must place in it only such a strictly qualified hope as would, even if it were to suffer complete shipwreck, leave his ultimate hope as securely anchored as before.

(*What is Christian Civilization?*, pp 53-56)

(F) *The Sacraments*

1 THE SACRAMENTAL UNIVERSE
by Donald Baillie

THERE is a very interesting passage in Calvin's *Institutes* in which he bases the Christian sacraments on this broader basis of nature, recognizing that God can take any one of his created elements and use it sacramentally, apart from the sacraments in the narrow and proper sense. As an example he takes the rainbow which, in the

Genesis story, was given to Noah and his posterity as a sign and pledge of the mercy and faithfulness of God. Now we in the enlightened twentieth century may very well ask: How can the rainbow really be a pledge of the mercy and faithfulness of God? We can indeed imagine primitive man after a deluge of rain seeing its beautiful spectrum suddenly appearing and stretching across the sky, and taking it as a blessed supernatural portent for his comfort and reassurance; but since we now know the rainbow to be a natural phenomenon of the polarization of light by moisture in the air, how can it prove anything about God at all? Let us not, however, imagine that Calvin was naïve and superstitious about it. With a touch of caustic wit he meets that point. 'If any dabbler in philosophy, in order to deride the simplicity of our faith, contends that such a variety of colours is the natural result of the refraction of the solar rays on an opposite cloud, we must immediately acknowledge it; but at the same time we will deride *his* stupidity in not acknowledging God as the Lord and Governor of Nature, who uses all the elements according to His will for the promotion of His own glory. And if He had impressed similar characters on the sun, on the stars, on the earth, and on stones, they would all have been sacraments to us .... Shall not God be able to mark His creatures with His Word, that they may become sacraments, though before they were mere elements?' (*Institutes*, Book IV, xiv, 18).

Here we have a recognition that because nature is God's and He is its creator, it lends itself to His use, and He can make its natural elements to speak sacramentally to us; not in the sense of a 'natural theology' which can *prove* the purpose of God from a mere contemplation of nature, but in the sense that God by His Word can use, and therefore we by our faith can use, natural objects, and some (like the rainbow) more naturally than others, as sacramental expressions of His mercy and faithfulness.

It is very much the same thing that we find in our Lord's use of natural objects as instruments of faith. The nature-parables of Jesus seem to be not merely passing illustrations of what He had to say, but something more. They depended on the fact that God is the God of nature, that the whole natural world is His and is fitted to speak to us of Him. Nor does this again mean that in the manner of natural theology we can find God in nature, take the facts of nature as giving us premises from which we can validly deduce God, or truths about God, as our conclusion; but rather that faith can use nature sacramentally. 'Consider the lilies of the field, how they grow; they toil not, neither do they spin: And yet I say unto you, That even Solomon in all his glory was not arrayed like one of these. Wherefore, if God so clothe the grass of the field, which to-day is, and tomorrow is cast into the oven, shall he not much more clothe you, O ye of little faith?' (Matthew 6:28-30).

If that were regarded simply as a syllogistic argument from the beauty of the wild flowers to the conclusion that there is a God who will take care of each one of us and provide for us, it would obviously be a very precarious argument, and no one ever came to believe and trust in God in just that way. Yet we may be sure that when Jesus uttered these words His mind was going back to moments when He had derived real comfort and strength for His faith from the contemplation of the flowers of the field, and the little birds of the countryside. His faith in God saw God's working, God's love and care, in the natural objects, and drew strength from the sight. To his faith these things became sacramental, just as long before in Israel, some Hebrew believer had looked at a rainbow until to his faith it became a sacrament of the mercy and faithfulness of God. It is only when God speaks and awakens human faith that the natural object becomes sacramental. But this can happen to material things only because this is a sacramental universe, because God created all things visible and invisible.

(*The Theology of the Sacraments*, pp 45-47)

2 INFANT BAPTISM
by Donald Baillie

SOME years ago I heard a woman lecturer on child psychology say something which immediately seemed to me to have a bearing on sacramental doctrine. She was speaking of a hospital for motherless babies in India, and how, for lack of a mother, many of the babies pined away and died, however well-fed and attended. The nurses, of course, kept the usual rule of not handling the babies unnecessarily, but letting them lie in their cots with a regular routine and the minimum of interference. But one day, she told us, an Indian woman walking about the ward and dandling a baby in her arms said, 'Why don't you let the nurses dandle the babies? *A baby must have love*'. The lecturer went on to explain how nothing can take the place of that physical way of communicating affection, the maternal touch, the actual loving contact of the mother's or the foster-mother's hand with the baby's body – 'epidermis against epidermis', and not for any purely physical reasons, but because 'a baby must have love', and only through that subconscious channel can the maternal love reach a child who has not yet any self-conscious existence at all.

When I heard the lecturer, I thought at once of the sacrament of baptism. If 'a baby must have love', it is also true that a baby must have the grace of God in order that it may grow as a truly Christian child. And it is through the faith and love of the Church and the parents, directed upon the child through physical channels, and using the effective symbolism of baptism, that the grace of God reaches the scarcely conscious child. And the half-unconscious trustfulness engendered in the child through this supernatural environment – is it not the beginning of the child's faith?

> *The Baby has no skies*
> *But Mother's eyes,*
> *Nor any God above*
> *But Mother's love.*
> *His angel sees the Father's face,*
> *But* he *the Mother's, full of grace;*
> *And yet the heavenly kingdom is*
> *Of such as this.*

~ Father John Banister Tabb ~

This is no sentimentalism, nor is it magic, but sacramental doctrine. Let us remember what the austere Calvin said about the purpose of the sacraments; that God in His wonderful providence has accommodated Himself to our capacity, because in this mortal life we are not purely spiritual beings like the angels, but live in bodies of flesh (*Institutes,* Book IV, i, 1). And to those who asked how infants without any knowledge of good or evil could be regenerated, or how faith, which 'cometh by hearing', could come to infants incapable of hearing the Word, Calvin replied that we must not limit the power of God, who works in ways we cannot perceive or understand, and who, to those incapable of hearing the Word, can give His grace otherwise (*Institutes*, Book IV, xvi, 17-19). Perhaps modern psychology has given us a clue beyond what Calvin could possess.

But the argument is not yet complete. There is something yet to be added for the full justification of infant baptism – something of very great importance. I may introduce it by quoting the following words from the Westminster Confession: 'The efficacy of baptism is not tied to that moment of time wherein it is administered; yet notwithstanding, by the right use of this ordinance, the grace promised is not only offered, but really exhibited and conferred by the Holy Ghost, to such (whether of age or infants) as that grace belongeth unto, according to the counsel of God's own will, in his appointed time' (chapter xxviii, 6). The latter part of the sentence covers what I have just been saying. But the first clause gives us something which I have not yet used in my argument. The point is that a person's baptism should be to him a means of grace, not merely at that moment but ever afterwards; and the faith which appropriates the grace offered in that sacrament includes the faith by which all his life long he looks back to his baptism.

So when the objector asks, 'How can an unconscious child have faith? and therefore why should he be baptized?' I reply 'Why do you assume that the faith must come first, or simultaneously? Are you forgetting that, just because a person is baptized only once, the faith which afterwards looks back to it is part of its very meaning?' That is entirely in line with our whole conception of what a sacrament is. A sacrament is a sacred sign which faith uses for its strengthening and growth. Or better: a sacrament is a sacred sign which God uses for the quickening of our faith. And in the case of baptism the sign is given only once in the life of the individual, but its *efficacy* continues working through faith as we look back. So Calvin maintains that infants are baptized into *future* repentance and faith, the seeds of which are implanted in their hearts by the Holy Spirit; and that according to New Testament teaching 'the thing signified' need not precede the sign, but may come after.

All this is, of course, in line with the principle laid down in the Westminster Directory of Public Worship that the adult Christian should look back to his baptism with understanding, and by faith use it as a means of grace.

It is deeply interesting to find in our own time Oscar Cullmann, as a New Testament scholar, on the basis of a careful examination of the conception of baptism present in the New Testament, coming to a conclusion which thoroughly bears out this position. According to the New Testament, on Cullmann's exposition, the background and presupposition of this sacrament is the general baptism for *all* men accomplished on Calvary. What happens in the actual administration of the sacrament is that the individual baptized is thereby set by God within the Body of Christ. In the case of an adult coming over from Judaism or paganism a declaration of personal faith is demanded of the praying congregation *during* baptism, but also faith is demanded *after* baptism of all who are baptized, and thus the efficacy extends through the whole subsequent life of the person baptized.

In that sense our faith is a response to what God does for us first on Calvary and then in our baptism. *God's initiative precedes our faith; our faith follows.* Surely it is in *subsequent* faith going on right through a man's life that, above all, the sacrament becomes efficacious and a channel of the grace of God. It is well known that Luther, throughout his life, when oppressed by the sense of sin and judgment, used to say to himself, for the encouragement of his faith: '*Baptizatus sum*, I was baptized.' And so, as Cullmann says, 'the complete baptismal event' extends through the whole life.

This raises the question so much debated in recent years of the relation between baptism and confirmation in the complete process of Christian initiation. Into that large question I cannot now enter. *But* if we of the Reformed tradition do defend infant baptism on the lines I have indicated (as I believe we must), then surely it follows that we must make much more than we have often done of the subsequent step, whether we call it confirmation or anything else, when the baptized person, having come to years of understanding, makes profession of faith and is admitted to full communion. For whatever else the individual does at that point, he ought to be laying hold by faith of what was given him as an infant in the sacrament of baptism.

(*The Theology of the Sacraments,* pp 86-90)

3 THE REAL PRESENCE
by Donald Baillie

IT seems very important to realize that the doctrine of transubstantiation itself was an attempt, however unsuccessful and unsound, to avoid crude and materialistic conceptions of what happens in the sacrament, and even to save the idea of the Real Presence from a crudely spatial interpretation. I owe my understanding of this to Canon Lilley's admirable little book entitled *Sacraments.* When the medieval divines, and finally St Thomas Aquinas, worked out the doctrine of transubstantiation, they were doubtless assuming an Aristotelian metaphysic of substance and attributes which we can no longer accept, but they were endeavouring to spiritualize a conception of the miracle of the altar which was already dominant in the minds of the people, and the result was far less 'materialistic' than we commonly suppose. When the Roman doctrine teaches that in the miracle of the altar the substance of the bread and wine is changed into the substance of the body and blood of Christ, while the 'accidents', the sensible qualities, remain unchanged, this does not mean that the body of Christ is locally or spatially contained in the bread, as it were inside it, so that if you peeled off the surface you would find the flesh of Christ. After all, according to the scholastic metaphysic, the spatial properties belong to the accidents, not to the substance. The substance (whether of the elements or of the body) is not, strictly speaking, in space at all. And therefore the Real Presence is not, strictly speaking, a *local* presence *in* the elements – even on the transubstantialist view. Surely what the Roman doctrine at its best is struggling (with a very inadequate metaphysic) to conceive is the reality and objectivity of the divine presence as something prevenient and given, if only we will accept it.

(Dom Gregory Dix says that the preoccupation of Western theology with the metaphysical problem of the relation of the elements to the body of Christ was a result of the medieval emphasis on *seeing* the action of the eucharist, since it could not be heard in the vernacular, as the words were in Latin (*The Shape of the Liturgy,* p 621). No wonder then, that the Reformers insisted that the sacraments must never be separated from the Word!)

And surely it is the same truth that we Presbyterians are endeavouring to express in a safer and surer way when we say that in the sacrament Christ is as truly present to the faith of the receiver as the bread and wine are to his outward senses. 'Present to the faith of the receiver' – that is the most real presence conceivable for a divine reality in this present world. The most objective and penetrating kind of presence that God can give us is *through faith.* Any other kind of presence, any local or spatial divine presence, if we could conceive it, would be less real, less besetting, less intimate. St Paul's prayer for his friends at Ephesus is 'that Christ may dwell in your hearts through faith' (Ephesians 3:17). That is how Christ dwells in men's hearts in this present world.

This does not mean that somehow we conjure up the divine presence by believing in it, or that we produce the faith out of our own resources and that in response to our faith God gives us His presence. Nay, God is prevenient, and faith depends on His actions; He calls it forth, and that is His way of coming to dwell in a man or a company of men. That is what He does when He uses the symbolism of the bread and the wine, the words and the actions, to give Himself to us in the sacrament of the Lord's supper.

Sometimes the question is asked (by people who are more

'evangelical' than 'sacramentalist'): Are we saved by faith or by sacraments? Surely that is a false antithesis and alternative. The truth is that we are saved by neither, but by God. But He saves us through faith, and therefore partly through sacraments, which He uses to awaken and to strengthen our faith. Thus the sacrament of the Lord's supper is indeed a means of grace, an instrument of salvation. And how can the Reformed Churches ever recover the meaning and potency of the sacrament until they approach it in that way? The danger is that in endeavouring to restore the power of the sacrament, we should strain ourselves to work up effects, to produce in ourselves devout and salutary effects, and thus in celebrating it to concentrate on ourselves, our own feelings, our own emotions, our own psychological states; which is the very opposite of what a sacrament should mean. The sacrament, by giving us not only words, but visible and tangible elements, should draw our thoughts away from ourselves to that great divine reality which is even nearer and more truly real than the things we can see with our eyes and touch with our hands. The Lord's supper is indeed the sacrament of the Real Presence.

But this leads us to a further stage of the argument .... A moment ago, in speaking of *faith* as the mode of the divine presence with us, I used repeatedly the phrase, 'in this present world'. We must now return to that phrase, because it reminds us of a situation which ... is of the very meaning of the sacraments. While the Lord's supper is indeed the sacrament of the Real Presence, it belongs also to a situation in which we are not in the 'immediate presence of God', and indeed to a situation in which we stand between a memory and a hope, looking backward to the incarnation and forward to the final consummation. We saw that the theology of our time has in various quarters come to a new understanding of the nature of the Church as belonging to that interim period; and that is immensely important for the sacrament of the Lord's supper. For the Real Presence in the sacrament is in a paradoxical sense a presence-in-absence. There is a sense in which, as St Paul puts it, 'we are absent from the Lord' (II Corinthians 5:6). His presence with us is not of the same mode as it was with His disciples in the days of His flesh, nor of the same mode as it will be when we come to see 'face to face' (I Corinthians 13:12). Thus it is of the very nature of this sacrament that it points back to the one and forward to the other.

On the one hand it is *a memorial feast*. None of the great Churches has ever reduced it to this alone, but each has always regarded this as part of its meaning. The Lord's supper must always be, among other things, in remembrance of Jesus Christ and particularly of His passion, and all its other meanings must depend on that historical reference; for it is an historical reference – the Church's corporate memory of the episode of the cross of Christ. Archbishop Brilioth remarks that the historical reference of the eucharist, as commemoration of an actual event, sharply distinguishes it from all such celebrations in the Greek mysteries where the historical actuality of the cult-story does not matter at all. It does matter vitally for Christianity, and the historical reference to the passion of Christ controls the whole meaning of the eucharist. St Paul says, 'As often as you eat this bread and drink this cup, you do show the Lord's death until he come' (I Corinthians 11:26). He may have meant that the action of taking and breaking the bread and pouring out the wine is a dramatic representation of the death of Christ, who, as he says elsewhere, had been publicly portrayed or placarded, as crucified, before the eyes of the Galatians (Galatians 3:1). But some scholars think the Greek word translated 'ye do show' or 'portray' ought to be given its more natural sense and translated 'You do announce' or 'proclaim' or even 'recite'. Thus the sentence may mean: 'whenever you celebrate the Lord's supper, you recite the story of the passion'. If so, it would indicate that in St Paul's time it was the custom to recite that whole story at the Lord's table, and this might well account for the fact that the part of the Gospel story which narrates the final scenes is out of all proportion fuller and more detailed than all the rest of the story; all the details were faithfully preserved because from the earliest days they were being continually recited in the weekly worship of the Church.

In any case that must always be a determinative part of the meaning of this sacrament. We do this because of what Jesus did with His disciples in the upper room in Jerusalem on the night before His crucifixion and we 'do this in remembrance' of Him, and particularly of His death. Christianity can never get away from the Jesus of history, and so the Church's corporate memory of Him must always be a vital part of its central act of worship, the Lord's supper.

But in this sacrament the Church has not only a present enjoyment and a memory of the past, it also has a looking forward into the future.

*   *   *

Here also is a remarkable and often quoted passage from C. H. Dodd, which has deep truth even for those who cannot accept his entire theory of 'realized' eschatology. 'In the Eucharist, therefore, the Church perpetually reconstitutes the crisis in which the Kingdom of God came in history. It never gets beyond this. At each Eucharist we are *there* – we are in the night in which he was betrayed, at Golgotha, before the empty tomb on Easter Day, and in the upper room where he appeared; *and* we are at the moment of his coming, with angels and archangels and all the company of heaven, in the twinkling of an eye at the last trump. Sacramental communion is not a purely mystical experience, to which history, as embodied in the form and matter of the sacrament, would be in the last resort irrelevant; it is bound up with a corporate memory of real events' (*The Apostolic Preaching and its Developments,* 1936, p 234f). Edmund Schlink also writes, 'In the Lord's supper we already share here on earth in that future glory. In the Lord's supper we are present at the death of Christ and at His return, at His first and second advent' (in *Intercommunion,* edited by Donald Baillie and John Marsh, 1952, p 296).

Such passages show magnificently how at this sacrament we have the presence, the memory and the hope all in one.

St Paul is plainly conscious of standing between that past and the future, between the memory and the hope, when he tells the Corinthian Christians what the Lord's supper is. 'I received from the Lord what I handed on to you, that on the night of His betrayal the Lord Jesus took bread, and when He had given thanks, He brake it and said; "Take, eat, this is my body which is broken for you; this do in remembrance of me .... As often as you eat this bread, and drink this cup, you proclaim the Lord's death *until He come*'" (I Corinthians 11:23-26). The early Church was most vividly and intensely conscious of living in that interval every time it met for worship and celebrated the supper; most intensely conscious of it because to them the interval appeared as a very short one. The thing they remembered from the *past* – the death of Christ – was in the very recent past, and many had seen His Cross with their eyes. And the thing to which they looked forward in the future seemed to them to be in the very near future – they thought the Lord was going to return in their own lifetime. The Church and the sacrament were indeed eschatological realities to them.

To us, perhaps, it is far more difficult to make that aspect real; partly, perhaps, because in certain sectarian quarters the very idea of a second advent has been used in foolish and sensational ways, and partly because even in the most responsible theological quarters the very word 'eschatological' has been used too much in recent years, and used even as a piece of jargon.

But surely it is profoundly true (as we said in a previous lecture) that the reason why we need this sacrament at all is because in this present world we are strangers and pilgrims, and all human history is a pilgrimage towards something that lies beyond, some supernal reality, a Kingdom of God in which sacramental symbols will not any longer be needed because God Himself will be its temple.

(The Theology of the Sacraments, pp 100-106)

(G) *The Christian Life*

1 OUT OF NAZARETH
by Donald Baillie

And Nathanael said unto him, Can there be any good thing come out of Nazareth? Philip saith unto him, Come and see.

~ John 1:46 ~

'CAN any good thing come out of Nazareth?' We don't know whether there was anything against Nazareth, any special reason why it should have been treated in such a slighting way, as a place where you wouldn't expect anything very beautiful to blossom.

There was nothing wrong with the situation of Nazareth: you can see it there yet, nestling in a little pocket on the side of a hill which commands an extensive and beautiful view. It wouldn't be bad for a child to grow up in such a spot.

But certainly Nazareth had never been remarkable for anything in the way of religion. It had never produced a great man, or a prophet, a man of God. It is never even mentioned in the Old Testament at all, which means that it hadn't any notable religious and historical associations. There weren't any heroic stories that could have been told about its past. Moreover, it was a little country town, and you know the saying that 'if God made the country and man made the town, the Devil made the little country town'. Nazareth may not have been any worse than the rest. It is Nathanael in this chapter who asks: 'Can any good thing come out of Nazareth?'

Well, you see, Nathanael himself belonged to the neighbouring village of Cana; and you know how it often is in a country district, how neighbouring villages are rather apt to look down on each other, so that even the guileless Nathanael was a little suspicious when Nazareth was mentioned – didn't think it likely that anything very notable and beautiful would hail from that quarter. He couldn't imagine the drab old village of Nazareth blossoming in such a way.

As a matter of fact, it was much the same with the people of Nazareth themselves: we discover that from another passage in the Gospels. Even they didn't expect Nazareth to produce anything very wonderful. No doubt they were fond enough of their village, and they wouldn't stand any nonsense about it from the people of Cana or any neighbouring village. But after all, life was pretty hard and secular in Nazareth. They felt it wasn't a place that would ever run very much to religion or heroism. They didn't expect that of themselves and they didn't even encourage it.

When one day Jesus, in the course of His ministry, went back to

Nazareth, where He had been brought up, He didn't get much of a reception. They said: 'He's just one of ourselves, he's a Nazarene, he was brought up in the village, and used to be a carpenter, and we've all employed him, and we know his people, his brothers and sisters – they're still in the village; and so *he* can't be much.'

They didn't expect their village to break any records in the way of religious goodness and greatness. They had known too much about commonplace days and commonplace ways in their mean village. Nazareth wasn't the kind of place in which it was easy to be good, or in which Heaven seemed near, or in which wonderful things would be likely to happen. That kind of thing wouldn't hail from Nazareth. How much of human nature there is in all that! Nazareth is not the only place of which it has been said. But Nazareth is the classical instance, because Nazareth is the place that has forever given the lie to all those dreary cynical negations and sceptical questions.

For out of Nazareth, out of dreary commonplace unlikely Nazareth, there did come, by God's grace, the greatest good that has ever come to mankind. In a humble home in Nazareth, unknown to the world, there grew up Jesus Christ. There He first learnt to walk and to talk, there He played with other boys, there He went to school, there He learnt his trade, from there He went forth at the age of thirty to kindle in the world a flame that is still burning and will never die.

It was a Nazarene that did that. His followers came to be called the Nazarenes. The name of Nazareth became dear with sacred meanings and is now enshrined in the heart of all mankind.

O sing a song of Nazareth,
Of sunny days of joy;
O sing of fragrant flowers' breath,
And of the sinless Boy.
For now the flowers of Nazareth
In every heart may grow;
Now spreads the fame of His dear Name
On all the winds that blow.

That is what has happened, by the grace of God, to the village of which once it was asked: 'Can any good thing come out of Nazareth?'

Now I want to tell you something in my own experience. Years ago in the course of a walking-tour, I was at a little English village called Mamble, on the uplands above the River Teme, on the borders of Shropshire and Worcestershire. I had never heard of it except in one place – John Drinkwater has a poem about it, and that made me curious to go and see it. Drinkwater had never been there himself, but the lazy sound of the name Mamble had tickled his fancy, and this is how his poem goes:

> I never went to Mamble
>   That lies above the Teme,
> So I wonder who's in Mamble,
>   And whether people seem
> Who breed and brew along there
>   As lazy as the name.
> And whether any song there
>   Sets alehouse wits aflame.
> The finger-post says Mamble
>   And that is all I know ...

And so on. I needn't finish it. But curiosity made me tramp along the road to Mamble, which Drinkwater imagined to be such a lazy sort of place. When I got there, there certainly wasn't much of it: a tiny little village, a few houses, one little shop, an old church, and a little inn.

The inn wasn't very hospitable – they couldn't give me a bed for the night. And it was rather noisy for a Sunday afternoon. I wasn't very sorry to clear out and go to a farmhouse outside the village. Mamble wasn't the sort of place one would choose to live in; it was a poor unpromising kind of village.

In the afternoon I walked along to the old village church – partly to find out if there was to be an evening service which I could attend. As I was standing in the doorway, looking around, a lady in black came in at the gate of the churchyard, carrying flowers. I thought she was going to put them in the church. But she walked past the church into the back part of the churchyard, and then I saw that she was putting the flowers on a grave. A few minutes later I spoke to her and asked her about evening service, and that opened a conversation. She was a farmer's wife. They were simple folk but they had sent their son to Oxford – the only one they had, as their other child had died young. This one was a six-foot youth of brilliant parts and evidently a heart of gold. He was their hope and pride. After three years at St John's College, Oxford, he had won a travelling scholarship in the interests of international friendship, and had spent a year in France and Germany. Then, just as they were expecting word as to when he would arrive home, they received a telegram to say that he had been accidentally drowned. This was the second anniversary – it had happened just two years ago that Sunday. Some of his friends from a distance were coming to attend evening service in memory of him, and she was putting flowers on his grave. She said he had some wonderful friends in Oxford, and also that he had remained quite simple and unspoilt. She said she believed in the end he would have become some kind of missionary, because his one dream was to use any gifts he had to do a little good in the world. His gifts must have been outstanding. But now that dream was over, and his father and mother had a grave to tend and a golden memory to keep.

That was in Mamble churchyard that Sunday afternoon. It gave one a glimpse of a home and a life, a dream and a memory. Perhaps you think that probably a mother's love somewhat gilded and glorified the picture. That may be. But when I think of Mamble now, it is not just of the lazy name in Drinkwater's poem, and the poor little village and the noisy little inn, but of that little church and churchyard, and that Sunday afternoon, and that story.

What a window it opens! Mamble was an unlikely place for anything notable to happen – lazy Mamble, a mere name on a fingerpost, a mean little village. But Mamble had its story to tell of the great simple human things: home, and hopes, and love, and death, and grief and memory; yes, and its story to tell of a keen young life that was given to noble aims and dreams, until it was cut off, or rather (shouldn't we say?) called to higher opportunities in realms unknown. Its training ground for all that was the little village of Mamble. That was where the boy learnt to love the home to which he always remained loyal; that was where he first went to school; that was where he thought the 'long long thoughts' of youth. All that had been going on in Mamble. 'Can any good thing come out of Mamble?' Of course it can; and there it was.

'Nothing very remarkable, after all,' perhaps you think. No, of course it wasn't very remarkable. The thing is the kind of thing that can happen anywhere – is happening everywhere. That is just what I want to tell you. I've told you that simple story, not that we may become sentimental over it (that would be a poor thing to do) but that we may take home its bracing lesson to ourselves, wherever we happen to live.

Almost every one of us knows what it is to settle down into a state of inexpectancy, a habit of not expecting very noble things of ourselves. Our life seems such a commonplace thing. The place we live in seems such an unhelpful place. The circumstances in which we are placed seem so unfavourable. We sometimes have a vision of what a truly noble Christian life would be – what it would be to live in this world as one of God's heroes, clean and brave and kind, a son or daughter of God, a knight-errant of his Kingdom. But all that seems very far away from us. It belongs to the time 'when knights were bold', or at least it belongs to more romantic places than the places where we have to live our lives. It belongs to people whose lot is cast more favourably than ours. As for us, what chance have we?

If we could make a new start somewhere else, we might have a chance, but what chance have we here where we are? (Perhaps we don't say all that to ourselves in words, but we say it half-unconsciously.) You don't expect very much of yourself. You hardly expect ever to be much of a Christian, to be a very good pure courageous unselfish man or woman. You hardly expect to be of much use to God or man. You don't take very seriously, as applied to yourself, the great offers and promises of the Gospel. How can all that happen in your unpromising life? Can any good come out of Nazareth?

And the answer is: Yes, it can. Out of Nazareth came Jesus Christ, the Son of God. And it was always His way to go here and there, to the most unlikely places, and seek out all sorts of conditions of men and women to make them kings and priests to God.

It might be Nazareth, or Bethsaida, or Jerusalem. And a little later it might be Ephesus or Corinth or Rome. And in our time it might be London or Mamble, or Glasgow or St Andrews, or any other place, where your lot is cast, or mine.

Let me ask two questions as I close.

(1) Is there anyone reading this who is going to do a great work some day for God? Well, of course, you can't answer. You don't know. After all, the main thing is not to do great things, but to do God's will. But this is the kind of thing I mean. God's Church on earth always needs foreign missionaries.

That is a great work. It is not profitable financially, it is not safe, it is not easy, it is not a good investment – it has nothing to recommend it except this: that it is better worth doing in itself than anything else in the world. It is unmistakably the work of God. I wonder if there is any one of you who will hear the call to it.

You parents, wondering what your sons and daughters will do when they leave school: what would you say if they told you they were going to be missionaries? Why shouldn't they? Why shouldn't your family provide such an offering to God? And you young people, why not you? In spite of all obstacles. Is there perhaps among you some David Livingstone, some Mary Slessor?

(2) My second question is even more searching: Is there any of you who does not want a place in God's great purpose? There isn't anyone who need be left out, unless you want to leave yourself out. Jesus Christ is 'able to save to the uttermost those who come to God by Him'. God's grace can work in every kind of Nazareth, every kind of life. Without His grace nothing good can come out of anywhere. But by His grace anything may happen anywhere. And His grace is not far from any one of us, to make our lives great and good, beautiful and useful, wherever our lot is cast, if only we will commit our lives to Him.

(Out of Nazareth, pp 1-8)

2 To the Obedience of Christ
by John Baillie

'Casting down imaginations [margin: reasonings], and every high thing that exalteth itself against the knowledge of God, and bringing into captivity every thought to the obedience of Christ.'

~ II Corinthians 10:5 ~

THIS text speaks of the conversion of the mind, and is, therefore, a good text from which to preach to a University audience. The conversion of the mind must indeed be part of every man's conversion. 'Thou shalt love the Lord thy God,' said Jesus, 'with all thy heart, and with all thy soul, and with all thy strength, and with all thy mind.' The mind is the citadel of the man, and Christ has not really won a man for Himself until He has conquered that citadel. No man is truly Christ's until his thoughts are Christ's. But these words of Christ were spoken, we are told, to a student of law, and there was accordingly special point in reminding him that he must love God with his mind. And this letter of St Paul was written to Greeks; and the Greeks, as he himself said, 'sought after wisdom', so that there was special point in reminding them that they must bring their thoughts into captivity to the obedience of Christ. Hence also these texts are of special importance for us University folk who devote so much time and attention to the things of the mind.

'Every thought,' the Apostle says. But there are two very different kinds of thoughts in the minds of us all. There are the little thoughts and there are the big thoughts; the fleeting fancies and the ruling ideas. Each has its own different and very great importance, so that it will be worth while to consider each in turn.

First, then, the little thoughts. Their name is indeed legion. They are more in number than the stars. I will not ask you how many thoughts you entertain in the course of a single day, but only how many sometimes pass through your mind in the course of a single minute – and I think that even then you will find it impossible to recapture. I know indeed, that if anybody were to ask you what you have been thinking about to-day, only one or two things would at first occur to you. They would be what I should call your officially acknowledged thoughts; they would no doubt concern matters of public or professional or family importance, and though not always very weighty, they would at least be eminently respectable. These are the thoughts that pass what the psychologists call the 'Censor'. But we know that our minds are also at all times giving hospitality to all sorts of unofficial contents. What was in my mind as I waited for the bus at the street corner? What visions did I see in the clouds of my tobacco smoke, as I leaned back in my chair to enjoy my after-dinner pipe? What were my thoughts when at last I went to sleep? And what my day-dreams during my idlest waking hours?

Now, as you know, there is nothing that recent psychology has so much impressed upon us as the importance of these little thoughts. It is in these thoughts, we are told, that the subtle secrets of personality lie concealed, the formation of character, the causation of nervous disorder, and even the border-line between sanity and madness. Indeed, if you consult a psychiatrist, he will use every means to ferret out your little and repressed ones. And it is very remarkable how our modern novelists and poets and even our modern painters have come, under the influence of this new psychology, to occupy themselves less and less with the big official thoughts that used to occupy the Victorian writers and artists, and are more and more concerned to reproduce the little thoughts – our dreams and our day-dreams, our flitting fancies, our random reveries and whatever else fills the little-noticed nooks and crannies, and the dim-lit marginal regions of our waking and sleeping life. Compare the Waverley novels with those of Proust or James Joyce or Virginia Woolf; compare the 'Idylls of the King' with 'The Waste Land'; compare a picture by Sir John Millais with a picture by Cézanne; and it will be evident how great a change has in this way been brought about.

I am indeed by no means convinced that the change is on the whole an improvement. I know at least that the literature and art it has produced are already beginning to pall on me and that I am more and more inclined to seek relief from it in the art and letters of an earlier day. No study of our little thoughts is likely to be either profitable or significant unless it is undertaken in the interest of big thoughts, and the defect of so much of this modern literature is just that, in the absence of ruling ideas of its own, it shares in the very triviality which it makes it its business to expose. Nevertheless, modern psychology serves a most useful purpose in explaining the mechanism by which our little thoughts affect the formation of personality, and in showing up the nature of the havoc they work on our minds when they are not properly controlled. It has explained this as it was never explained before, yet the fact itself is something that wise men have always understood. As, for example, that wise man, Marcus Aurelius, who, in his little book addressed to himself, once jotted down these words: 'The soul is dyed the colour of its leisure thoughts.'

But now if this is true, if the soul is really dyed the colour of its leisure thoughts, then it is clear that a man is not really converted until his leisure thoughts are converted. I may have given my full assent to all the doctrines of the Creed and have no doubts concerning any of them, I may have so re-ordered my life in accordance with Christ's commands as to fill my whole day with blameless and charitable deeds; but what Christ wants of me is something much deeper than intellectual assent and moral conformity. He wants me to be born again as a new creature. He wants a radical transformation of the very sub-soil of my mind, so that there is no longer any hidden poison at the roots of my overt thoughts and actions ready to work its ravages at the first favourable opportunity. He is, therefore, as interested in my idle moments as in my busy ones, as much in my reveries as in my resolutions, as much in my castles in the air as in the more solid edifice of my public and professional life. No man is really Christ's until his day-dreams are Christ's – aye, and his night-dreams too, if they are anywise subject to his control. 'My soul,' wrote the Psalmist, 'shall be satisfied as with marrow and fatness; ... when I remember thee upon my bed, and meditate on thee in the night watches.' Or again, 'Commune with your own heart upon your bed, and be still'.

When sleep her balm denies,
My silent spirit sighs,
    'May Jesus Christ be praised!'
When evil thoughts molest,
With this I shield my breast;
    'May Jesus Christ be praised!'

Something like this, then, is what is meant by bringing into captivity every little thought to the obedience of Christ.

But I must now pass to the big thoughts, because in this particular context it is the big thoughts that St Paul has most in mind. 'Casting down reasonings,' he writes, 'and every high thing that exalteth itself against the knowledge of God.' When a man seeks to submit himself to Christ, there is a danger that not only his very little thoughts but also his very big thoughts may escape the process of submission. The former are so trivial, but the latter are so general, that both may escape our Christian vigilance. And yet no man is really Christ's until his very biggest thoughts are Christ's. This letter of St Paul, as I have said, was sent to an address in a Greek city, and the ancient Greeks were famous above all peoples who lived before or since for their high structures of reasoning, for their great generalisations, for their love of ultimate principles and ruling ideas. The very word 'idea' comes from them, and the word 'philosophy' too. The history of philosophy begins with them, as every student knows; and nearly every variety of philosophical theory that exists in the world to-day was first thought of in ancient Greece.

It is obviously these Greek speculations and philosophical systems that St Paul here has in mind, and what he says is that they, too, must be brought into captivity to the obedience of Christ. Now I have myself been a student of philosophy all my life, and I well understand the temptation to believe that, if only I surrender to Christ my actions and my passions, I can keep my philosophy for myself, as it were in a separate compartment of my mind. But do you remember how G. K. Chesterton says in his book on *Heretics* that it is more important for a landlady to know what her lodger's philosophy is than to know what his income is?

Not that his income is unimportant. The poor widow who puts a card in her window must indeed satisfy herself that the stranger who pulls her bell must be able to pay for his lodging. But, says Mr Chesterton, to know his philosophy is more important still. And he adds that 'for a general about to fight an army, it is important to know the enemy's numbers, but still more important to know the enemy's philosophy'.

So it is with Christ. He is concerned with my daily habit of life and my daily habit of worship, but He is no less concerned with my philosophy. He knows that I am not fully and securely His until my philosophy is His as well. Therefore he wants my philosophy also to be transformed by the power of the Cross, and to be born again, and to repent in dust and ashes. Nor will He be satisfied till this has happened to all my reasonings and to every high thing that exalts itself in my mind.

You see, when Christianity first came to that old Mediterranean world, it found the great Greek philosophies already in possession. Every educated man followed one or other of the philosophic schools. This man would be a Platonist, this other an Aristotelian, the third a Stoic or a Pyrrhonist. And there is no question that each of these systems is really a towering intellectual structure, a massive and imposing attempt to survey all time and all existence, and to see all things together in a single view. Moreover, there is in them so much precious truth and insight that after two thousand years our minds still feed on them, and must continue to do so. It was therefore natural and inevitable that when an educated Greek in a city like Corinth was converted to Christianity, he should try to understand his new Christian faith and experience in the light of what he had already learned from his Greek masters. He would see whether there was not that in his Platonism or in his Stoicism which would help him to understand what had happened on Calvary and what was now happening in his own heart and life. Thus it fell out that the great intellectual conceptions discovered by the Greeks were pressed one after another into the service of the Cross, providing much of the intellectual framework for Christian theological reflection. Nevertheless, if it was to adapt itself as it ought to this glorious new filling, the framework must itself be radically transformed. The Greek philosophies had their legitimate Christian use, but not until they too had undergone Christian regeneration and conversion. They must first be baptised into Christ and humbly repent beneath the shadow of His Cross. They must be buried with Him in His death, before they could rise with Him into the newness of their Christian life. And if you read St Augustine's *Confessions*, you will see this process taking place under your very eyes. In other books you may read how Roman power submitted itself to Christ's yoke, but in this one you will read rather of the submission of Greek wisdom. Elsewhere you may read of the conversion of ruling monarchs, but here of the conversion of ruling ideas.

But now the danger of which St Paul here shows himself to be aware is that this process is not going to work out as it should. He is afraid that these Corinthians will merely try to pour the new wine into the old bottles. He is afraid that some of their ruling ideas will remain unbaptised, and the pure Gospel of Christ be corrupted or curtailed by being forced into this pre-Christian frame. And he knows that Christ cannot be sure of His triumph in Corinth while there is one high thought that has not been rendered obedient to Him.

Nor, alas, was his fear without foundation. There is no doubt that from the second century onwards the Christian Church suffered from the tendency to build into the structure of its Christian thought this or that untransfigured element of paganism. And, speaking as a student and teacher of theology in these latter days, I should say that we are still haunted by the same danger. Instead of viewing all things in the light of Christ and His Cross, Christian thinkers still tend to view Christ and His Cross in the light of other things. Instead of allowing our Lord to determine the whole of our philosophy, we too often allow our philosophies to determine Him. We try to find room for Him within a world-view that we have constructed without His help, and to understand Him by means of such ruling ideas as were in our minds before He came to us, or before we came to Him. There are men whose deeds are done beneath the shadow of the Cross, but who, when they begin to think, prefer to walk some distance away from it – sometimes a very great distance – in order, as they explain, to get the Cross itself in better perspective. But the experiment is a difficult one. The Cross has always seemed a queer object when seen from afar. It refuses to fit into any distant landscape. It refuses to soften into the background of any picture. Either it is out of perspective itself, or else it puts everything else out. 'Unto the Greeks foolishness,' wrote St Paul in his former letter to this same Greek Church.

For myself, I am increasingly convinced that most of our modern difficulties of belief find their origin in this situation. We are so departmentalised in our outlook. We want to be Christians, but we are not prepared to let Christ rule in every region of our thought and life. We surrender our Sunday thoughts to his obedience, but on week-days we give our obedience elsewhere. We try to have one set of ruling ideas for our religion, but perhaps another for our citizenship, and still another for our study. In our study of history, for example, we too often divest ourselves of our Christian knowledge before we address ourselves to the understanding of historical events. It is of course true that a proper autonomy must be allowed to all our science and historical research. But nowadays this autonomy is often allowed to extend itself to the ruling ideas by which each and all of these interests are ultimately governed. Yet a wise man once said that 'there are no ultimate principles in politics', and I believe it to be equally true that there are no ultimate ideas in science or historical research. The ultimate ideas which we bring to bear on these interests are always supplied from the central citadel of the mind: and if we are truly Christ's, then in that central citadel it is Christ who must be King.

Let us, therefore, consecrate not only our most trivial fancies to the Lordship of Christ, but also the master thoughts that guide us in our studies. If I may so express it, let us not leave our station on Calvary either when we don our carpet slippers, or when we don our thinking caps. Only thus can we cast down all reasonings, and every high thing that exalteth itself against the knowledge of God, and bring into captivity not only our very smallest, but also our very biggest thoughts to the obedience of Christ.

(University Sermon in the *Cambridge Review*,
December 1944, pp 134-135)

3 THE RELIGIOUS LIFE
by Donald Baillie

And in the morning, rising up a great while before day, he went out, and departed into a solitary place, and there prayed.

~ Mark 1:35 ~

It is told that just before the Battle of Edghill in 1642 General Sir Jacob Astley prayed with his army the following simple prayer: *O Lord, thou knowest how busy we must be this day: if we forget thee, do not thou forget us; for Christ's sake. Amen.* That, I think, is a good parable of how the religious life has to be lived amid the hustle and bustle of a workaday world.

And now here is another prayer illustrating the same thing, by a man with a very different kind of occupation. It was Dr Thomas Arnold, the famous Headmaster of Rugby School a century ago, who used this prayer every day regularly: *O Lord, we have a busy world around us. Eye, ear and thought will be needed for all our work to be done in the world. Now, ere we again enter upon it on the morrow, we would commit eye, ear and thought to Thee. Do Thou bless them and keep their work Thine, that as through Thy natural laws our hearts beat and our blood flows without any thought of ours for them, so our spiritual life may hold on its course at those times when our minds cannot consciously turn to Thee to commit each particular thought to Thy service: hear our prayer for our Redeemer's sake. Amen.*

I think these two little stories set before us very plainly the whole problem of how a man is to be religious when there are so many things to attend to in this world. How can you be religious all the time? That is the problem. And I think these two stories give us not only the problem but also the solution. The religious life is not a matter of retiring from the world altogether and giving all one's time to the thought of the divine. But it does depend on finding time in our busy lives for the quest of God in prayer – as that general knew and that great schoolmaster also.

Now it is just the same thing that is illustrated in such a clear and beautiful way in the passage I have taken as our text. And in this passage it is the very case of Jesus Christ Himself. It was all true for Him also – for Him who, as we say, lived in the very bosom of the Father, but who also lived amid the world's work and play. Just notice what it is that we find described in this chapter. Jesus had had an exceedingly busy day, from morning till night – in the morning a very straining and exciting time in the synagogue in Capernaum; then immediately after, a case of sickness to deal with in a private house, the mother-in-law of Simon Peter; and then at evening a whole crowd of people thronging around the door of the house clamouring to be relieved by Jesus. And he did what he could for them. Then it was bedtime and Jesus and his disciples were very ready for it. But when the disciples awoke next morning and looked around for their Master, He was not in the house at all. Long before daybreak He had got up and gone out, when all was quiet. He had needed rest and sleep for His body, but He needed something else too. He needed spiritual refreshment for His soul, and He could only get it in solitary prayer. And so we have to picture Him yonder on the hillside under the waning starlight and the first streaks of dawn, when no one else was abroad, throwing His soul open to the influences of God in meditation and prayer.

The disciples had hardly seen that sort of thing before, and they were rather puzzled by Jesus. Why had He gone out there alone? They went out and found Him. They said to Him, 'All the people are looking for you.' And He said: 'I must go on into the next towns and preach there also; for that was why I came forth.' And so there was another day opening out before Him. It was going to be busy and noisy, people would be crowding around him. Eye and ear and thought would be occupied. But through the noise and dust and distraction of it all Jesus would be living as in God's presence, His spiritual life holding on its course, because in those quiet hours of the early morning He had turned His soul to God upon the lone hillside.

There in the perfect religious life you have the picture of the alternation of leisure and work, prayer and activity, the eternal and the temporal. That is how the religious life can be lived in this workaday world.

Now I want in the light of all that to lay down two simple truths about it.

(1) *The religious life does not mean that you will be thinking about religion all the time.* That is impossible. There are plenty of other things in this world that need to be attended to. We all have our work to do, and we have to be thinking of that most of the time – unless we are thinking of it we shall not do it very well. General Astley had to fight his battle. Dr Arnold had to teach his school. Everyone has his task to perform. Jesus Christ had His mission to carry out amid the dust and toil of those towns of Galilee; and even He couldn't be directly thinking of religion all the time.

Now of course there have always been in this world some people who thought that you couldn't be really religious unless you retired from the world altogether into a life of holy seclusion. One can quite well understand that idea and how it has sometimes appealed to enthusiastic souls. Religion seems such a sublime spiritual unearthly thing, and so exacting in its demands, that you haven't very much chance of getting deep into it unless you give all your time to the pursuit of it, without any secular occupation or interest at all. So some people have felt. And thus, with a longing for the religious life, they have forsaken the world and become monks or nuns and lived apart from ordinary mankind that they might live nearer to God. That sort of thing can be seen throughout the course of religious history.

It would be a poor thing for us to condemn all that; for that monastic life has throughout the Christian centuries produced a great many real saints, and has given to the world hymns and books of devotion that will never be forgotten. And yet somehow we can't help feeling that that cloistered or hermit kind of Christianity is very different from the kind of life lived by Christ our Master. He lived a busy human life among the haunts of men. There were, indeed, in His time, as in every other time, good men who retired like hermits from the world. There was John the Baptist, for whom Jesus had such an admiration. John lived in the wilderness. He preached to the people indeed, but they had to go out to the wilderness to hear him. He lived a strange ascetic life, clothed in camel's hair, eating locusts and wild honey – a quite different life from what his ordinary fellow creatures were living in the towns and villages of Galilee.

But Jesus lived among men, moved about among them and shared in their activities, their social joys and sorrows; going as a guest to all sorts of houses, taking part in wedding feasts, carrying on his beneficent work in their towns and villages; so that people even used to contrast Him with John the Baptist, and to say that Jesus was everybody's companion. He had many things to think of, many people to talk to, much distraction, much occupation for ear and eye and lip and mind. And it was in these circumstances that He lived the perfect religious life. He was living the eternal life amid the things of time.

That is, I say, the real lesson of the religious life. We know that we have to love the Lord our God with all our heart and soul and strength and mind. But that does not mean that we are to be interested in nothing else. That does not mean that we are to be thinking of religion all the time. Nothing could be falser than that idea. For the main thing is not to be thinking about religion, but to be living it. That is the real thing we have to learn, to live constantly in a religious spirit amid the common tasks and distractions and social intercourse of daily life in this workaday world. When we can do that, then we have the happiness of being religious men and women.

It is rather a notable thing that even that Catholic Church of the Middle Ages which gave such honour to the monastic life has so many beautiful stories that teach us that the unselfish active life among men is somehow best of all. Do you remember the story of St Basil and the Gooseherd? St Basil was one of the pillar-saints. He lived day and night for many years on the broad top of a stone pillar forty feet high, praying for his own sins and the sins of the world. Then one night an angel came to him, took him down to the ground and said: 'Follow this road to the third milestone, and there you will find a man who can instruct you, because he is well-pleasing to God.' When Basil got to the third milestone he saw nothing but a flock of geese approaching, herded by a rustic man with a little girl. Basil told him he had been sent to him by an angel for his soul's good. But the gooseherd didn't know what he meant. He had spent his life herding the geese and taking care of the little girl, an orphan whom he had found. That is all the story. And that was the man from whom the holy St Basil of the Pillar had to learn the secret of the religious life.

Friends, these stories must be welcome truth to us. For we have to live in a workaday world and carry on our common occupations. Of course we can't be always thinking about religion. But we can live the religious life through all our occupations if the right spirit is in our hearts.

(2) *The religious life does depend on your having certain times for meditation and prayer.* It can't be that all the time; it is not desirable that it should be; it is into the workaday world that we have to bring the atmosphere of the divine. But we can't bring it into the workaday world unless we sometimes steal aside from the noise and toil and ascend the mountains of the spirit to breathe the atmosphere of the divine. That was what the general did before his battle. That was what Dr Arnold did before his day in school. They couldn't be thinking of God all the day through their exacting tasks. But they could think of Him and pray to Him at the beginning of the day: and that would set them right at the start and keep them right all through. That is what religious men and women have always done, until almost as a matter of course it has become part of the religious life. And that is what Jesus did too. Indeed I suppose Jesus is the original pattern of that kind of thing in religion – at least in the matter of private prayer. In His time religion was pretty much a public matter. To go off in the early morning to a quiet hillside spot for prayer seemed to the disciples such a novel thing. I suppose the reason why Jesus chose the hillside was partly because no privacy or solitude was possible in one of those tiny village houses of the Galilean peasants, and partly perhaps because Jesus found it easier to lift up His heart to God in the open air and under the open sky, for He was a lover of nature. But the reason why He did the thing at all was because He knew by experience that without that way of beginning the day, without that periodic interval of devotion, it is impossible to keep on living in a religious spirit amid the distractions of the world.

Now that has in the Christian era become a regular part of the religious life. But, after all, how easily it slips out of the religious life – at least out of many lives that profess to be religious and dimly mean to be so! It seems such an idle thing in this busy world to stop and give any time to a matter like the cultivation of the spiritual life. It is so easy to go upon one's way and tell oneself that work is as good as prayer and duty is the best religion and so on, until one has really become weary and worldly at heart without knowing it; just through losing the sense of divine things by the neglect of the spiritual life. For one does soon lose the sense of divine things. It is impossible to keep it, it is impossible to carry the atmosphere of God with one through the common days of toil and care, unless we sometimes stop to breathe that atmosphere in the quietness of a moment of devotion.

Friends, I am sure there are many lives into which a new beauty and inspiration would come if they would only learn to make a habit of that kind, a personal habit of religious devotion. And I am sure there are many homes (even Christian homes) into which a new beauty would enter if they would only revive something of the Christian custom of family worship which is not as common in Scotland as it used to be. What a difference it might make for your whole day if every morning your thoughts and prayers did for a moment turn to God! And what a difference it might make to the whole life of your home if every day there were heard in it, read aloud in the presence of all the household together, the words of a chapter of Scripture, psalm or prophecy, or the wonderful words of our Master in the Gospels.

Don't you think that then in our towns there would be more of the atmosphere which Jesus carried about with Him through the towns and villages of Galilee long ago?

(Out of Nazareth, pp 115-121)

4 To Pray and not to Faint
by John Baillie

And he spake a parable unto them to this end, that men ought always to pray, and not to faint.

~ Luke 18:1 ~

THE parable in question is that of the importunate widow. It represents our Lord's teaching about prayer in what many would regard as its extremist form. Nowhere in the religious literature of the world can we find stronger statements about the power and efficacy of prayer than we find in the preaching of Jesus, and this parable of the importunate widow has often been felt to be the strongest statement of all. Jesus is here telling us what we are to do when we have prayed and prayed again and our prayer has apparently not made the slightest difference to anything. And what He does is not to offer us any alternative method of obtaining our desire, but simply to say, 'Go on praying all the harder, all the more importunately'. To give point to this advice He asks us to think of the most unpromising human analogy we can find – the case of a poor woman without any standing or influence in the community appealing for redress to an unjust judge who 'feared not God, neither regarded man'. Could there be a more hopeless case? She has appealed many times, but the judge will not move a finger to help her; what more can she do? She can do nothing, says Jesus, but appeal again – and yet again; until at last she tires him out and he says to himself, 'I will avenge her, lest by her continual coming she weary me', or, as may very likely be the true translation, 'lest she end by scratching my eyes out!' Could there be a stronger statement than that of the efficacy of importunate prayer?

St Luke tells us that the moral of this parable is that men ought always to pray and not to faint. The word *faint* will, however, come to many people to-day as a surprise. We are so apt to interpret the meaning of prayer as if Jesus had said that men ought always to pray and not to *work*. That, I believe, is precisely the mistake that most of us make in our thinking about prayer: we think of it as an alternative to effort. We often speak as if there were two contrasted ways of facing the evils of our mortal lot – we may either fold our hands and pray about them, or we may pull ourselves together and do what we can to mend them. And standing as we do in the tradition of what the philosophers call Western activism, you and I are almost sure to regard the latter as the nobler and manlier way.

But it is quite plain that our Lord's way of looking at prayer is as different from this as the day is from the night. What he said was that men ought always to pray and not to *faint* or, as the modern versions have it, not to *lose heart*. That is to say, he regarded prayer, not as an alternative to effort, but as an accompaniment of effort and an alternative to despairing acquiescence and inaction. In His language, and indeed in the language of the whole New Testament, the opposite of praying about a thing is to do nothing about it at all, and the opposite of working for a cause is to stop praying about it. Prayer unaccompanied by hard work and work unaccompanied by urgent prayer are two things that Jesus Christ not only never preached but never even contemplated as a plausible possibility. He knew well that the men who worked most tirelessly were not likely to be a different set of men from those who prayed most importunately, but the same set of men. And indeed history bears this out in the fullest possible way. It is not the philosophies of reforming zeal, but rather the philosophies of quietistic resignation, that have found no place for prayer in their schemes. Buddha, who founded the great religion of acquiescence in the East, was probably the first teacher in the world who taught his disciples that they must not pray. The Stoic teachers, who founded the great Western philosophy of acquiescence, did exactly the same. The Stoics would have been profoundly shocked by this parable of the importunate widow. Indeed all our Lord's teaching about prayer would have shocked them. To keep *asking* God for things, they would have said, means that one is not yet resigned to what His will appoints. 'We should come to God without any previous desire or aversion,' writes Epictetus the Stoic, 'just as the wayfarer asks the man he meets which of two ways leads to where he is going, not wanting the right hand to be the way rather than the left; for he wants neither, but only that which leads him to his goal .... And what is best but just what pleases God? Why then do you do all you can to corrupt your judge and pervert your counsellor?' And Spinoza, the greatest modern philosopher of acquiescence, has precisely the same teaching.

Could anything be *less* like the teaching of Jesus than that? *He* had little enough hesitation, not only in making His desires known to God, but in asking and begging and importuning God to grant them. 'Ask ... seek ... knock' – that is His trinity of imperatives. Prayer is for Jesus not nearly so much connected with resignation as it is with *rebellion*. In that fine book with the striking title *The Faith that Rebels* the late Principal Cairns of Aberdeen points out that practically all that is said in the New Testament about prayer is said not in the interest of being reconciled to things as they are but in the interest of getting things changed.

Let us then consider one or two remarks that one hears currently made about prayer, and bring them to the test of this saying of Christ's, that 'men ought always to pray, and not to faint'.

Sometimes we say, 'I am working so hard these days that I have no time to say my prayers'. That sounds like an excellent excuse; God can hardly blame us for not seeking His presence when it is the exigencies of His own service that are keeping us away from Him. Yet I wonder whether this excuse is often very sincere. Is it really the doing of God's will that is robbing us of our hour of prayer? Would more prayer really mean less work? I have a suspicion that often it is not the quantity of work we do that makes us too tired to pray, but the amount of worry we expend on it. We moderns like to think of ourselves as terribly busy – that again is part of our so-called 'activism'; and certainly we have the appearance of being busy enough. A modern city street, a modern office, a modern railway station undoubtedly give the impression of such activity as would have made our forefathers gape with astonishment. But I doubt if we are really as busy as we look – or at least if we are *doing* as much as we seem to be doing. Reinhold Niebuhr says in one of his books that, 'The modern urban man, shuttling between his office and his apartment, is hardly as significant a person as a traditional peasant in his village community' – and the peasant was never so busy that he had not time to pray. A Spanish writer says even more pointedly that the life of a nun in a bare cell is more genuinely intense and active than that of a New York business man. And though the nun's life may not be our ideal of the highest life, I think we must admit that he is right in his comparison. After all a person who is too busy to pray will also be too busy to think; and what is the good of labour that is not guided by constant thought about its meaning and its end? Prayer, after all, is but thinking towards God. And I believe Jesus would have said that all deep and proper thought about our work must be directed towards God and so be of the nature of prayer. He would have said that all the good we do is done by God in us and through us. Even of Himself He said, 'I can of mine own self do nothing'. But there we go again, thinking of prayer as an alternative to work, whereas Jesus thought of it as an alternative to *fainting,* an alternative to *losing heart* in our labours and so failing to get anything effective done at all. I am quite sure that if only we did not set about our daily round so unthinkingly, so unprayingly; if only we gave more time to the practice of inward recollection; if only, while we are actively occupied with our tasks, we were more conscious of doing them in God's presence and by the aid of His divine grace, we would not only get more real work done, but we would do it with less expense of spirit, less weariness, less worry and less anxiety. 'Men ought always to pray, and not to faint.'

Take again another remark that I recently heard a man make. 'If prayer is reasonable at all,' he said, 'it should be confined to the great spiritual issues of life. We should not pray about little things. We should not trouble God about our trifling earthly affairs.' What would Jesus have to say to that? I'm sure He would have said that if anything is big enough to *worry* about, then it is not too small to *pray* about. Of course, if you are so high-minded a person that little things never worry you, then certainly there is no reason why you should worry God about them. That was exactly why the Stoics of old would not pray. They had persuaded themselves that they were, as they put it, 'indifferent to all outward goods and evils'. They tried to believe that nothing worried them, and nothing mattered, but the inward state of their own souls. I am afraid the poor Stoics usually bluffed themselves in this matter, but perhaps you are really the kind of man they tried so hard to be – the world's first successful Stoic. Perhaps the little things of earth never occupy your thoughts at all. There is no doubt that that is a most enviable state of mind, if you really possess it. Did not Jesus Himself bid us take no thought for such things as food and drink and clothing, and seek first the Kingdom of God and His righteousness? Ah yes, but He went on to say something else too. He said, 'Your heavenly Father knoweth that ye have need of all these things'. He said 'All these things shall be added unto you' – and there is a world of difference between this confidence that God will supply our needs and the Stoic's pretension that it does not matter whether our needs are supplied or not. If you never worry over the lesser things and the earthly things, then you are a remarkable exception, and very different from the rest of us – as our Lord well knew. I am afraid the common case with those who do not pray about the little things of life is that they worry about them all the more. It's not a question of whether we *ought* to worry over these things, it's a question of whether we *do* worry over them. And I'm afraid we do worry over them terribly; we lie awake at night turning them over in our minds; they spoil our peace of soul; they make us grow old before our time. Well then, says Jesus, tell your worries to God. 'Your heavenly Father knoweth' – He knows, but He wants you to tell Him. He wants you to keep nothing back from Him that is in your mind at all. In prayer there must be no reserve. Surely it is a false shame that keeps you from confessing what no true shame keeps you from thinking. Surely it is a false pride that keeps you from praying about things which no true pride prevents you from worrying about. It is futile to enter God's presence pretending to be more high-minded than we really are. 'Ye people, pour out your hearts before Him' – that is what Scripture says. And can one imagine anything more futile than a man praying with his *lips* to God for inward salvation of his soul, when in his heart he is all the time worrying about something quite outward and earthly – about the health of his body, or about how to make ends meet in the feeding of his family? No wonder Jesus spoke a parable unto the multitude to this end, that men ought *always* to pray, and not to faint! Or as it was put by St Paul in writing to the Philippians: 'In *nothing* be anxious; but in everything by prayer and supplication with thanksgiving let your requests be made known unto God.'

Take finally another remark. 'Surely,' one sometimes hears it said, 'it is absurd to try to change the will of God. Who are we that we should tell God what to do? If we believe in God at all, we must believe that he is already ordering all things for the best.' Well, let me say first that Christian prayer is not telling God what to do; it is rather telling him what we think we need. It is 'making our requests known unto Him'. In the last resort Christian prayer has always left it to God's own wisdom to decide what precisely He is to do about our need. With all his importunity the Christian never ventures to *dictate* to the Most High: he always adds, 'If it be Thy will'. If I thought that God were going to grant me all my prayers simply for the asking, without ever passing them under His own gracious review, without ever bringing to bear upon them His own greater wisdom, I think there would be very few prayers that I should dare to pray. Just as I believe my boy would not dare to beg things of me as importunately as he sometimes does, if he thought I was going to grant them even against my better judgment and without discrimination. He would feel, and rightly feel, that the responsibility thus thrown upon his immature judgment was far too great to be borne. 'This,' we read in the New Testament, 'is the boldness that we have toward Him' – not that if we ask anything we like He will cause it to happen; no, but – 'that, if we ask anything according to His will, He heareth us'.

But there is something else to be said. You do not pray, you say, since you believe that God must know best and that therefore He is already ordering all things for the best. Well, if you believe that, then you have indeed attained – attained at least to a very lofty Stoicism, if not to quite the whole of Christian wisdom; but *do you really believe it?* You see, if you really believed that God were ordering all things for the best, then you would not only stop *praying* for things you have not got but you would also stop *wanting* them. There is neither piety nor logic in continuing to want things for which, on the ground that God knows best, you have stopped praying. Ought we, for example, to stop praying for the recovery of our friend from sickness on the ground that God knows best? Obviously we should not consider that a ground for ceasing to *work* for his recovery – to work for it by every available means which modern medicine has set at our disposal. And if it be right to work to that end, how can it be wrong to pray? Clearly we must not pray for any end towards which it is wrong to labour, but likewise we must not labour towards any end for which it is wrong to pray. There is nothing more soul-destroying than to be filled with anxious hankerings which are kept back from God. At the root of half our human tragedies lie worries that have never been resolved into prayers. 'Men ought always to pray, and not to faint.'

Is there someone here who will never be a good Stoic? Is there someone who altogether fails to face his lot with an equal mind? Are you near to fainting? Near to losing heart? Are you overborne with labour? Or worn out with worry? Or consumed with hopeless longings? Then won't you take your Lord's advice? Don't try to keep the whole thing pent up within your own heart. Share it with God. Tell him all about it, yes, down to the last and absurdest annoying detail. 'In *nothing* be anxious; but in everything by prayer and supplication with thanksgiving let your requests be made known unto God.' 'And He spake a parable unto them to this end, that men ought always to pray, and not to faint.'

(Christian Devotion, pp 20-27)

5 ELIJAH UNDER THE JUNIPER TREE
by Donald Baillie

But he himself went a day's journey into the wilderness, and came and sat down under a juniper tree; and he requested for himself that he might die; and said, It is enough; now, O Lord, take away my life; for I am not better than my fathers.

~ I Kings 19:4 ~

THE Sunday after Easter is commonly called Low Sunday. It is not quite certain what the origin of this name is, but some have connected it with the familiar fact that in living the Christian life we sometimes pass from the mountain-top to the low valley. Easter Day, when we remember the victory that God has given us in Christ, is the high point of the whole Christian year; and because we cannot always remain on the heights, because moods change, and reactions come, and exaltation may be followed by depression, Easter Day is followed by Low Sunday.

But whether that has anything to do with the origin of the phrase or not, there is no doubt that for a great many people the

Christian life does have these changes of mood and temper, those reactions, those bad hours. Therefore I think it may be useful to-day to consider for a little how we ought to deal with them. And that is why I have taken the story of Elijah under the juniper tree, utterly dejected and praying that he might die.

In the case of Elijah this did come just after the highest moment of his life, his triumph over the priests of Baal on Mount Carmel. That was indeed the victory of faith, and at the end of that chapter we find him dancing in prophetic ecstasy. And now, after the victory, comes the reaction, the depression, the doubt whether his work was of any value at all, and whether the cause of God had any future. We see him going off into the desert and throwing himself on the ground under a juniper tree, and saying: 'It is enough; now, O Lord, take away my life; for I am not better than my father.' That was his black hour. And that picture of Elijah under the juniper tree is a kind of timeless image and symbol of what so many of us experience now and again – of our times of depression, when the taste goes out of our life and out of our religion, when God becomes unreal and it is difficult to pray to him or to enjoy him.

What is the meaning of these moods? What ought we to think about them? How ought we to face them and deal with them?

To begin with, we must make sure that we have not, ourselves, created the cloud that is hiding God from our eyes. Perhaps we have created it by disobedience. Perhaps we are running away from God and from His will, and that is why we cannot enjoy the light of his countenance. Perhaps it is partly true even of Elijah that his gloom was due to his having run away into the wilderness, away from difficult duty, away from God's will. Anyway, God came and asked him: 'What are you doing here, Elijah?' And then God sent him back to where he had fled from, and told him what he had to do. But, whether this is quite true of Elijah or not, it is sometime true of Christians that they are themselves to blame for their times of gloom, because they are running away from God. And before we go any further, we must make sure of that point and put right what is wrong.

But of course that is not always the reason. And having dealt with that, I want now to go on to give you some simple bits of encouragement and counsel for those times when you are under the shadow of the juniper tree.

(1) Remember that *this is part of the common experience of the Christian life.* You are not different from others. You are not the first. We have started from the case of Elijah, away back in ancient Israel. But it is still more striking to note that this kind of experience is common right through the story of Christianity. It is indeed rather wonderful to discover how many of the great Christian saints and masters of the spiritual life tell of the times of dejection and desolation through which they passed. It has been so common an experience that it came to have special technical names attached to it. Sometimes it was called the experience of desolation (the opposite of consolation), and sometimes it was called 'spiritual dryness', because it felt so like being in a dry and thirsty desert where there are no springs of water. For example, St Francis de Sales, after speaking of the fine weather of religious joyfulness, goes on:

> *But this fine weather will not always continue; but sometimes you will find yourself so absolutely devoid of all feeling of devotion that your soul will seem to you to be a fruitless barren desert in which there is no pathway to find her God, nor any water of grace to refresh her, because of the dryness which seems to lay her entirely waste.*

It is then a widespread and common experience, very familiar even to those saints and masters who have gone far beyond what most of us have ever attained in the practice of the Christian life. These masters tell us what to do with our bad moods, and I am coming to that in a moment. But meantime I think it is a real help to discover the mere fact that the experience of days of depression has always been a common one among Christians, and thus, as it were, to clasp hands across the centuries with others, with fellow-Christians of all generations, who have passed through it too. So I say: Remember that for your encouragement.

(2) Remember that *what really matters in the Christian life is not our feelings, our emotions, our moods, but how we live,* with dedicated wills, in faith and love. And thus we ought to be looking away

from ourselves and our own feelings to God above us and our fellow-creatures around us. A great many people make the mistake of judging their religious life by the state of their feelings, by whether they are enjoying it or not, whether they can always take delight in praying to God and worshipping Him. And so, when they experience bad hours, in which God seems far away and all inspiration and joy seem to have departed, they are unduly discouraged. But that is really an elementary mistake. That is not the way to deal with our moods. Our feelings are bound to change. Our moods are sure to vary, just like the weather. But the Christian life must go on, independently of all the variations in the weather of our souls.

Of course there ought to be also in our Christian lives the days of a clear sky and the divine sunshine. But it is not by concentrating on ourselves and our feelings that we shall get the weather of the soul to come right in that respect. No, it is rather by forgetting ourselves, and performing our routine duties. What a blessing it is that in our uninspired hours there are the hum-drum duties that can be faithfully carried out without inspiration, and our fellow-men around us to whom we can be loyal and considerate even when we are depressed ourselves. But above all, let us remind ourselves that the great reality of God does not change with our changing moods. Even if at certain moments we cannot feel His presence, we do believe in His unchanging reality, in His eternal love, in what He has done for us through Christ, in His unfailing purpose of good. If we keep firm hold of these great realities, or rather let them keep firm hold of us, yielding our wills to God's will, then our feelings and emotions will take care of themselves. Or rather, God will give us such feelings, of consolation or desolation, as are good for us. He does not change. He is there, in all His blessed reality, behind the clouds that hide Him. He may be very near us just in those hours when we cannot feel His presence at all.

(3) In your bad hours, remember the *fellowship of your fellow Christians*, and lean upon it. That is half the meaning of the Church of Christ. We are far too apt to live the Christian life in a kind of proud loneliness and independence, with a 'lone-wolf' kind of religion. But that is not what Christianity was ever meant to be.

That is not how Christian gladness, as you find it in the New Testament, is generated. From the beginning Christianity was a rich and warm fellowship, and its joy was the joy of a beloved community. While you are walking by yourself in lonely brooding, there are doubtless others around you doing the same. And how much you could help them and they could help you if you took more seriously the comfort of the fellowship that ought to exist in the Church of Christ!

When Elijah lay under the juniper tree, in the depths of depression, he thought he was the only faithful Israelite left who had not fallen away to worship false gods. But God told him: 'I have yet seven thousand in Israel who have not bowed the knee to Baal', and he sent Elijah back into the service and fellowship of that church of the faithful. And God speaks to us in our depression and tells us to get away from lonely brooding into that mutual sharing of burdens and responsibilities, of joys and sorrows, of thought and worship, which is the very life of the Church of Christ, where 'brother clasps the hand of brother, stepping fearless through the night'.

I want to sum all this up by reminding you of a splendid passage in the *Pilgrim's Progress*, where Bunyan deals in his allegorical way with exactly the situation we are considering this morning; and undoubtedly he is drawing upon his own experience. I mean the passage about Christian the pilgrim going through the valley of the shadow of death. When Bunyan put that into his allegory he was not thinking of the actual death of the Christian, but of the experience of spiritual darkness, through which many a Christian has sometimes to pass. As the pilgrim was passing through this dark valley groping his way, he became so confused that he did not know the sound of his own voice, and when an evil spirit jumped on his shoulder and whispered blasphemous thoughts into his ear, he thought they came from his own mind. He was utterly disconsolate. And now comes this passage:

When Christian had travelled in this disconsolate condition some considerable time, he thought he heard the voice of a man, as going before him, saying: 'Though I walk through the Valley of the Shadow

*of Death, I will fear none ill, for Thou art with me.' Then he was glad
and that for three reasons.*

*First, because he gathered from thence that some who feared God
were in this valley as well as himself.*

*Secondly, for that he perceived God was with them, though in that
dark and dismal state; and why not, he thought, with me, though by
reason of the impediment that attends this place, I cannot perceive it?*

*Thirdly, for that he hoped, could he overtake them, to have company
by and by. So he went on, and called to him that was before; but he
knew not what to answer for that he also thought himself to be alone.
And by and by the day broke; then said Christian: 'He hath turned
the shadow of death into the morning.'*

Yes, the morning comes. The dark night of the soul does not
last for ever. And so, while it lasts, we can say to ourselves in the
words of another ancient Psalmist:

*Why art thou cast down, O my soul?
And why art thou disquieted within me?
Hope thou in God, for I shall yet praise Him,
Who is the health of my countenance and my God.*

And now unto God the Father, God the Son, and God the Holy
Ghost, be ascribed in the Church, as is most justly due, all honour,
glory, might, majesty, dominion and blessing, world without end.

(*To Whom Shall We Go?*, pp 151-156)

6 GRACE AND GRATITUDE
by John Baillie

IN the Bible the two concepts of worship and service are a single
concept. The Greek words for service (*latreia* or *leitourgia*) are also
the Greek words for worship. When we speak of worship nowadays
we think first of going to church, and when we speak of service we
think first of going out into action in God's world. But that this

dichotomy is a modern one is still evidenced among us by the fact that we at the same time retain from the older tradition the habit of speaking of our acts of worship as 'divine service', 'morning and evening service', *Gottesdienst* and so on; as well as by the fact that we speak of the form of our worship as the liturgy (*leitourgia*). This word was originally applied to any form of public service or office in the State; St Paul himself speaks of the rulers of the State as 'God's liturgists' (λειτουργοι θεου) (Romans 13:6), and he uses the word also for works of Christian beneficence and charity (II Corinthians 9:12; Philippians 2:17,30). Hence, if we do persist in our differentiated modern usage, we must at the same time remind ourselves that our worship of God is part of his service and our service of his worship.

* * *

I have felt that few explanations and reminders to be a necessary preamble to the point I am principally desirous of making, namely, that gratitude is not only the dominant note in Christian piety but equally the dominant motive of Christian action in the world. Such gratitude is for the grace that has been shown us by God, and again it is significant that gratitude and grace are hardly more than two forms of the same Latin word. Very often when I am present at a luncheon or dinner party, and especially when I am the only ordained minister of religion in the company, I am given a certain duty to perform, but in calling upon me my hosts do not always use the same words. Sometimes it is 'Will you say grace?', sometimes 'Will you return thanks?', and sometimes 'Will you ask a blessing?' This variation of phrase, usually with little or no variation of intended meaning, indicates the close relationship between the three concepts of thankfulness, grace and blessing.

In classical Latin there is of course no such word as *gratitude,* the simple *gratia* having to do duty for thankfulness as well as for grace; and in the Greek of the New Testament there is only the one word *charis* which in our English versions has to be rendered in some contexts as 'grace' and in others as 'thanks'. This may seem confusing, and indeed our translators frequently disagree as to which word to use in a particular passage (*eg* Hebrews 12:28, where the Authorised Version has 'let us have grace', and the Revised Standard Version 'let us be grateful'); but in fact it is illuminating as pointing to the close connexion between the two meanings – between the spring of God's action towards us and the spring of our response to Him. Again our words 'thank' and 'bless' very often translate the same word in the Hebrew of the Old Testament (*barak*). And when Psalms 103 and 104 have 'Bless the Lord, O my soul', and the three following have 'O give thanks unto the Lord', the meaning is the same, though in the latter cases another word is used (*yadah*).

But though the single word *charis* has to do duty not only for grace but also for thanks, there is another New Testament word formed from the same root but slightly different in meaning and usage, so that it appears in our English versions as 'thanksgiving' rather than 'thanks'. This is the word *eucharistia*, so familiar to us as the name of the central act of Christian worship, the Eucharist. 'The Lord Jesus the same night in which he was betrayed took bread: and when he had given thanks, he brake it ...' (I Corinthians 11:23). Here the phrase 'when he had given thanks' represents only a single word in the Greek original, the word *eucharistesas*. Thus the central rite of the Christian liturgy is a rite of gratitude. It is also a rite and liturgy of remembrance, for our Lord went on to say, 'This do in remembrance of me' (I Corinthians 11:24). But we remember in order to give thanks, as is already made plain in the Old Testament where it is in psalms of thanksgiving that we come upon such declarations as 'I will remember the works of the Lord'. And what is thus true of the Christian worship is also true of the whole Christian life. It is a life of remembrance which issues in thanksgiving. A true Christian is a man who never for a moment forgets what God has done for him in Christ, and whose whole comportment and whole activity have their root in the sentiment of gratitude.

There is nothing of which I am more firmly persuaded than that this is the right attitude to life. It is precisely in regard to such a conviction as this that I feel able to speak of certitude, and to do so without the least scruple or diffidence. Our natural tendency is to take the good things of life for granted, but to grumble when things do not fall out as we would wish. That is because we set out from a complacent view of our own worthiness, our own deserts. But the beginning of wisdom is to realize that such a view is without any foundation in reality. I am reminded of a conversation which I had many years ago with a certain excellent lady in America who came to see me to say that she had entirely lost the Christian faith in which she had been brought up. She could, she said, no longer accept any of the comforting beliefs on which Christians so confidently leaned; and then I remember the very words that followed: 'It seems to me that we mortals have no claim on the universe. We have no right to expect anything. We cannot say that we deserve anything.' Well, I thought how exactly right she was. To think like that is not yet to be a Christian, but it is to have a mind open to Christian truth. To have surrendered our own claim to a good thing is to be ready to recognize it as a free gift if and when it comes.

* * *

In this as in other things our Lord Himself has given us the perfect paradigm. His whole demeanour was one of thanksgiving to the Father, just as before partaking of the last meal he ate on earth, ευχαριστησεν – He gave thanks. Here He was following the invariable and prescribed custom of His own Jewish people, but at the same time foreshadowing the solemn Christian rite. The tract *Berakoth* (blessings) in The Talmud says, 'It is forbidden to taste of this world without saying a blessing: only the unfaithful do so'. No less full of thanksgiving are the letters of St Paul, who sometimes finds the most surprising occasions for it. Canon T. R. Milford, for instance, has drawn our attention to the fact that the Apostle can hardly begin a letter without thanking God for his correspondents. The exceptions are Galatians and Second Corinthians, and 'To receive letter from St Paul which did not somewhere near the beginning thank God for your existence, your conversion and your faith was a sure sign that you were in disgrace' (*Foolishness to the Greeks*, 1953; a little book from which I have borrowed more than this).

When, following our Lord's example, we give thanks before the breaking of the bread at the Eucharist, we are in the first place giving thanks for the bread itself. Like Him we are saying a grace before meat, for it is likely that the words He used were those on which He had been brought up. 'Blessed be thou, Lord God, eternal King, who bringest forth bread from the earth.' Here I am reminded, though quite incidentally, of having in my student days listened to a sermon by that prince of Scottish preachers who was then Principal of my own college, Dr Alexander Whyte, in which he declared that there was no more significant difference between a man and a brute beast than that, while dogs and pigs attacked the food presented to them with greedy and unreflecting taste, human beings will often be observed to bend their heads for a moment before setting to, and that in that little inhibition, that moment of pause, our sole human dignity resided.

But of course in the prayer of thanksgiving before the Fraction in our service of Holy Communion, we are expressing our gratitude not only for the food God provides for our bodily needs, but above all for the Bread of Life here symbolized and betokened, for the great salvation that has come to us all through the breaking of the Bread that was our Lord's Body. All other blessings are seen in the context of this supreme blessing, and all other thanksgivings are contained in this central eucharistic action; as in the words of our General Thanksgiving, 'We bless Thee for our creation, preservation, and all the blessings of this life: but above all, for Thine inestimable love in the redemption of the world through our Lord Jesus Christ'. Nor must it be forgotten that our prayer is said in the full realization that Christ is there with us as we pray. It is an act of grateful recognition of His real and personal presence in our midst.

(*The Sense of the Presence of God*, pp 235-241)

7 MORNING PRAYERS
by John Baillie

L ET me now go forth, O Lord my God, to the work of another day, still surrounded by Thy wonderful loving kindnesses, still pledged to Thy loyal service, still standing in Thy strength and not my own.

Let me to-day be a Christian not only in my words but also in my deeds:
Let me follow bravely in the footsteps of my Master, wherever they may lead:
Let me be hard and stern with myself:
Let there be no self-pity or self-indulgence in my life to-day:
Let my thinking be keen, my speech frank and open, and my action courageous and decisive.

I would pray, O Lord, not only for myself but for all the household to which I belong, for all my friends and all my fellow workers, beseeching thee to include them all in thy fatherly regard. I pray also –
for all who will to-day be faced by any great decision:
for all who will to-day be engaged in settling affairs of moment in the life of men and nations:
for all who are moulding public opinion in our time:
for all who write what other people read:
for all who are holding aloft the lamp of truth in a world of ignorance and sin:
for all whose hands are worn with too much toil, and for the unemployed whose hands to-day fall idle.

O Christ my Lord, who for my sake and my brethren's didst forgo all earthly comfort and fullness, forbid it that I should ever again live unto myself. Amen.

(*A Diary of Private Prayer,* Twenty-eighth Day)

*   *   *

CREATOR Spirit, who broodest everlastingly over the lands and waters of earth, enduing them with forms and colours which no human skill can copy, give me to-day, I beseech Thee, the mind and heart to rejoice in Thy creation.

    Forbid that I should walk through Thy beautiful world with unseeing eyes:

    Forbid that the lure of the market-place should ever entirely steal my heart away from the love of the open acres and the green trees:

    Forbid that under the low roof of workshop or office or study I should ever forget Thy great overarching sky:

    Forbid that when all Thy creatures are greeting the morning with songs and shouts of joy, I alone should wear a dull and sullen face:

    Let the energy and vigour which in Thy wisdom Thou hast infused into every living thing stir to-day within my being, that I may not be among Thy creatures as a sluggard and a drone:

    And above all give me grace to use these beauties of earth without me and this eager stirring of life within me as means whereby my soul may rise from creature to Creator, and from nature to nature's God.

O Thou whose divine tenderness doth ever outsoar the narrow loves and charities of earth, grant me to-day a kind and gentle heart towards all things that live. Let me not ruthlessly hurt any creature of Thine. Let me take thought also for the welfare of little children, and of those who are sick, and of the poor; remembering that what I do unto the least of these His brethren I do unto Jesus Christ my Lord. Amen.

                    (*A Diary of Private Prayer*, Thirtieth Day)

(H) *The Last Things*

1 JOURNEY'S END
by John Baillie

WHAT then of the individual's place within this heavenly Kingdom? When this question is asked, we notice that the Biblical authors first understand it with reference to those who will still be living on earth, when the end of history comes and the Day of the Lord dawns. Such of them as on earth have been true pilgrims will then pass into glory. But what of the generations that have already passed away and are now sleeping the sleep of death? In the ancient world the sleep of death never meant *extinction,* though nowadays that is the meaning often read into the phrase; the dead were conceived to be still in existence in an underworld – Hades or Sheol – though their existence was of so inert a kind as fitly to be described as sleep. What then of the pilgrims who are thus asleep? This was the last question to be asked. The Old Testament has hardly anything to say about it, and the earlier parts of it nothing at all. However, in the period between the Testaments it came to be most actively canvassed, and the New Testament provides us with a clear answer. In what is probably the earliest of all the New Testament documents St Paul writes: 'But I would not have you to be ignorant, brethren, concerning them which are asleep, that ye sorrow not, even as others which have no hope. For if we believe that Jesus died and rose again, even so them also which sleep in Jesus will God bring with him' (I Thessalonians 4:13-14).

Many of the further questions that we should like to ask are not answered for us by the New Testament or, where they are answered, it is in a highly symbolic and poetical way. But one thing is clear from its first page to its last – that all true pilgrims who meanwhile had died will rise again to share equally with the saints of the final generation in the things which eye hath not seen, nor ear heard, neither have entered into the heart of men to conceive. To know that is to know enough.

I know not where his islands lift
    Their fronded palms in air;
I only know I cannot drift
    Beyond His love and care.

        ~ Whittier, 'I bow my forehead in the dust' ~

Can we believe this? Is it reasonable confidently to cherish such a hope? To this my first answer must be that it would be quite unreasonable to cherish either this hope or any hope at all apart from belief in God. Indeed, I have gone further, and have argued that our minds are little likely to be open to the entertainment of the Christian teaching either as to present salvation or as to final glory until we have first purged them of all romantic illusions as to what man can do in his own strength. But if we do believe in God, then it seems to me that no *further* act of faith is here demanded of us. Christian faith does not consist in believing a number of unrelated things, but in surrendering ourselves to a single act of trust in the God and Father of our Lord Jesus Christ. If we do that, then the other things follow, and among them this: 'In my Father's house are many mansions' (John 14:2).

For to the narrower question whether it is reasonable to believe that the God and Father of our Lord Jesus Christ should by his almighty power receive into His heavenly Kingdom the souls He has redeemed through His beloved Son, I must reply by asking whether it would not be highly unreasonable to doubt it. The question is simply as to what the Christian faith implies in regard to the status and value of the individual human personality. Are we to think that individual human beings do not matter in God's eyes? I would put it to you that this is the very last doubt that should be raised in our modern minds, since it is on the Christian brethren that the whole of the Christian ethic is founded; and the Christian ethic – that is, the Christian way of treating others – is the one part of Christianity of which something survives in practically every modern soul.

(*Invitation to Pilgrimage*, pp 119-121)

2 THE KINGDOM OF GOD
by John Baillie

IF the Kingdom of God means simply the transfigured and per-fected order of human society which some day in the far-distant future will at last be realized, then it is only *the last generation* that will enjoy its blessings. And what of the generations that perish by the way? It is here that the development of Jewish and Christian thought, in close agreement with the thought of the Greeks, parts company with our contemporary futurism. It came to be felt, as we saw, that the Kingdom of God, if it is to be a satisfying object of hope, cannot be a mere earthly paradise (Revelations 21:1) to be enjoyed by the final generation, but a transcendent order of being in which all generations have a part. The Jewish teaching was that, when the Kingdom came, the righteous dead would share equally with the final generation in the blessings of its appearing. But where are they meanwhile? To this question there were three pos-sible answers: (a) that they remain, awaiting revivification, in the virtual non-existence of Sheol – as it were 'asleep'; (b) that they are in some intermediate state – as it were of incomplete blessedness; and (c) that they are already enjoying the blessings of the Heavenly Kingdom, having been admitted into it immediately after death, though not until the end of history will they be conjoined to their own bodies, and the cup of their blessedness be full. All three views are represented in the apocalyptic books (see Paul Volz, *Judische Eschatologie von Daniel Akiba*); and no clear agreement was ever reached.

But the very uncertainty has behind it an important grasp of truth. For here we have an attempted synthesis of the two one-sided views which we have been concerned to distinguish. Within the framework of a grand-scale philosophy of history room is being made for a philosophy of the single soul. There is a con-summation for society and a consummation also for the individual: and yet the two consummations are not two but one (Volz, op cit). Even here and now (so it has come to be felt) I as an individual in the presence of God, *solus cum solo*, may begin to live the eternal life of the Heavenly Kingdom; and after release from the present life I shall enter into the fullness of its joy; and yet can my joy be full, while perhaps my friends still live on earth and I am separated from them, while our human society lives a broken and divided life, while the company of the redeemed remains incomplete? The Christian Church has steadily replied that it cannot. Its teaching, both Roman and Protestant, has been that *there can be no complete consummation for the individual until there is consummation also for society.* This is the real significance of the conception of 'the Last Day'. It is not really for the sake of the 'Judgment' that 'the Last Day' is important, for it is taught that men will be judged and (except, for the Roman Church, in the case of those who must pass through purgatory) sent to their final destination, *at death,* so that the Great Assize is no more than, as we might say, a public announcement of a sentence that has already, except in the case of the final generation, been passed and put into effect. But the ortho- dox teaching, both Roman and Protestant, is that until the last day the souls both of the blessed and of the damned remain *disembodied,* though already dwelling in what is to be their final place of abode; but that on the Last Day there will be a General Resurrection whereby the souls of both are reunited to their old bodies. This, of course, *had* to be taught, so long as it was also taught that in the life eternal we are to have the same bodies of flesh and blood and bones (though rendered incorruptible) that we now possess; because these bodies were known to be meanwhile in the graves where they were buried. But the true significance of the teaching comes out only when we are told that the spirits of the blessed, though now enjoying the heavenly bliss *substantially,* will not pos- sess it in the fullness of its *accidental nature* until after the Last Day; for the deepest reason of this delay is not really that until then they will be disembodied, but that until then their society will be incomplete.

(*And the Life Everlasting,* pp 248-250)

3 UNIVERSAL RESTORATION?
by Donald Baillie

SOME months ago I visited a great steel works, and looked into the white heat of a blast-furnace, out of which the molten steel was pouring in a white-hot stream, so scorching that one could only view it from a distance. I said to myself that that was the kind of thing that had given men the conception of a Hell which was a lake of fire, as symbolizing the most dreadful punishment conceivable. But I also reflected that the purpose of that burning heat in the blast furnace of the steel-works is not destruction but purification and construction. The iron ore is freed in that heat from its impurities and so transformed that it can be shaped into things that are useful, reliable and beautiful. And that is also what can happen to the souls of men. They can be re-made, by the omnipotent love of God, which is a consuming fire, burning away all evil. But it may be an agonizing process, and most of all for those who are most impenitent and most unwilling to be turned to God. That is how it seems to me we may venture to think of the redeeming work of God as continuing even in realms beyond this present world. Does not that at least relieve some of the difficulties of the more traditional view? The traditional view that all those who do not turn to God in this present life will suffer everlasting punishment. That implies that God keeps them in existence simply in order to punish them. For if we do not believe that the human soul is essentially immortal, if we believe (as we must) that the very existence of every creature depends each moment on the will of God, then the orthodox view means that God raises the wicked from the dead and keeps them in existence, not in order to win them, but in order to torture them forever. Impossible. *But* if God continues his saving activity beyond death, can we go on from that to the doctrine of *Universal Restoration?* Can we take that further step? If God does give further opportunities beyond the grave to impenitent souls, if His love still seeks them out to make them penitent, and if His love is everlasting and omnipotent, is it not sure to win its way in the end in the lives of all men? How could such love ever give anyone up and shut the door of mercy? And how could such love be defeated in any human life? Therefore, it may well be asked, are we not driven to the conviction that in the final consummation of God's purpose all evil will be overcome, and all men will be gathered into His family, in a universe from which all sin and suffering will be banished, and God will be all in all? Is that the conclusion of the whole matter? Any other conclusion may seem unworthy of our Christian belief in the infinite and omnipotent love of God and in its redemptive power. Any other conclusion would seem to imply that *God has to give some men up*, either in the sense that there comes a point when God ceases to be merciful towards a persistent sinner, or in the sense that God's love is defeated by certain men, and will always continue to be defeated by these men, so that He has to accept defeat. But if God is infinite love, it is difficult to think of Him as ever ceasing to love any man, however long the man may remain impenitent; and also it is perhaps difficult to think of that going on forever without result, because the infinite love of God must ultimately melt the hardest heart into penitence, it cannot fail or be defeated. Are we then driven to believe that there will be a universal restoration?

That is certainly a very tempting conclusion, and it is one which has been accepted by many Christian thinkers. For example, it was entertained as a possibility in the early period by Origen of Alexandria (who even entertained the possibility of the Devil being ultimately redeemed by the love of God). Through the centuries there were occasional holders of the Universalist doctrine, though it was off the main track of orthodoxy. But it was in the 19th century above all that this doctrine had its effloescence; and at least the *possibility* of universal restoration was entertained by so diverse a crowd as: Schleiermacher, Erskine of Linlathen (the great Scottish lay theologian), Frederick Denison Maurice (who was a friend of Erskine's), Martineau (the Unitarian), and some of the Victorian poets, notably Tennyson.

> *(That nothing walks with aimless feet,*
> *That not one life shall be destroyed,*
> *Or cast as rubbish to the void,*

When God hath made the file complete.)

And perhaps it is not so much in conflict with the New Testament as we often suppose. It is true that as the end of the parable of the Last Judgment it is said of those who are on the Judge's left hand: These shall go away into everlasting punishment; and elsewhere we read, doubtless in a figurative sense, of 'everlasting fire'. And I am not going to argue, as has often been done, that the Greek adjective *aionios* does not mean everlasting, but agelong, for that would be a doubtful exegesis ....

But it has sometimes been pointed out (*eg* Hobbes) that the idea of everlasting punishment or everlasting fire does not necessarily imply that any one individual will remain forever in that torment; and in any case these occasioned parabolic and apocalyptic expressions are not sufficient to justify the basing of a dogma upon them. But further, it has often been pointed out that in some passages, St Paul seems, with a wide sweep of Christian hope and vision, to entertain the prospect of a universal restoration of all things in Christ, a redeemed universe from which all evil shall have been removed. In the philosophy of history which he gives in the 11th chapter of the epistle to the Romans, where he speaks of the hardening and the blindness of the Jews, he seems to regard it as a step towards a merciful consummation – 'until the fullness of the Gentiles be come in, and so all Israel shall be saved'; and 'God has shut up all into unbelief, that he might have mercy upon all' (Romans 11:25:32). Cf also: I Timothy 2:4f, 'God our Saviour, who would have all men to be saved and come to the knowledge of the truth'. And in Ephesians 1:10 Paul(?) speaks of God's great purpose of 'consummating all things in Christ', which suggests universal restoration. Still more remarkable is the difficult passage in I Corinthians 15:22ff, 'For as in Adam all die, even so in Christ shall all be made alive .... Then cometh the end, when He shall deliver up the Kingdom to God, even the Father, when He shall have abolished all rule and all authority and power. For He must reign until He hath put all His enemies under His feet ... and when all things have been subjected to Him, then shall the Son also himself be subjected to Him that put all things under Him, that God may be all in all'. That has sometimes been interpreted as giving or implying a picture of universal restoration.

And yet I think it is a doubtful exegesis, and I do not think the evidence generally justifies us in attributing to St Paul a definite doctrine of universal salvation. (For one thing, it is quite possible that what he really believed in was *conditional immortality*.) Even if Paul did picture a final consummation in which all evil would be wholly extinguished from the universe (which is doubtful), that does not necessarily mean universal salvation: it might mean that the universe would be set free from all evil through the ultimate extinction of *rebellious* and impenitent souls (including the Devil – his hosts?). That would give us the doctrine of *conditional immortality*, which has been maintained by many Christian thinkers: the doctrine that only redeemed souls are immortal, while the impenitent will pass out of existence altogether. Hints of this are in Justin Martyr, Irenaeus; more definitely in Arnobius (beginning of 4th century). In Reformation era it was held by the Socinians (as in the Racovain Catechism, 1605), and it is said that even such a high churchman as Bishop Jeremy Taylor regarded it as not inconsistent with the Christian faith. During the 19th century: Armand Sabatier, Lyman Abbot, Henry Ward Beecher, R. W. Dale, James Young Simpson (died 1934). This need not mean, of course, that the existence of the unredeemed comes to a final end when their bodies die: it might be held that their existence goes on beyond death, and that they have still for long ages the opportunity of coming to repentance, but that ultimately if they are impenitent they will pass out of existence and be utterly extinguished.

Now it cannot be denied that a good deal can be said in favour of that doctrine of *conditional immortality*. In some ways, indeed it seems to fit in particularly well into the New Testament world of thought. I do not think, as I have already said, the New Testament anywhere shows any trace of the idea that the human soul is essentially and inherently immortal, so that it cannot pass out of existence – though that idea ultimately came into Christian teaching, doubtless from Greek philosophy. The New Testament speaks of the end of the wicked as *destruction*. Jesus speaks of God as 'Him who is able to *destroy* both soul and body in Gehenna' (Matthew

10:28) and He spoke of those who shall lose their souls or their lives (Matthew 10:28, 16:26b), and his parables of the Tares and the Dragnet may well be taken to suggest that the fate of the wicked is like the destruction of refuse. (Though we must always remember that a parable is a parable and that it is dangerous to press the details.) St Paul speaks of the wages of sin as death, while eternal life is the gift of God to the redeemed. Similarly the Johannine literature conceives of 'eternal life' as the gift of Christ to His own people. 'They shall never perish' (John 10:28). 'He shall never perish' (John 10:28). 'He that believeth on me, though he were dead, yet shall he live (John 11:25). 'He that doeth the will of God abideth for ever' (I John 2-17). All of this may well be taken to imply that those who do not do the will of God, those who are not united to Christ, do not abide for ever; that there is no natural or inevitable or universal immortality, but only an eternal life which is given by God to the faithful; while the rest will pass out altogether in the end, having counted themselves unworthy of eternal life. Obviously there is a strong element in New Testament thought that seems to ask for a doctrine of conditional immortality.

And yet the picture is not quite clean and sure. It must be remembered that in the New Testament, particularly in Johannine writing, 'eternal life' means much more than simply continued existence: it means a rich quality of living in the knowledge of God through Christ, a thing which in a measure may be enjoyed even now; so that those who miss it do not necessarily pass out of existence altogether. Thus it can hardly be said that any doctrine of conditional immortality is clear and explicit in the New Testament. And regards general theological considerations, it has its difficulties. For here again, we are involved in the idea of God giving certain men up altogether, and not merely in the sense that His love continues indefinitely to be defeated by their impenitence, but that there comes a point when, as it were, He give it up as a bad job and lets them perish out of existence. I should find it very difficult to adopt that as a dogmatic position.

But neither should I find it easy to adopt a doctrine of universal restoration as a dogmatic position. For to hold dogmatically that all men will and must finally be saved does seem to reduce the significance of the choice which every man has to make. I do not mean that it makes salvation too easy, for even on the universalist view it might be far from easy: it might come to an individual through countless ages of suffering, and the longer he resisted, the more he would suffer. But if a human choice is involved, is it not possible that a man should continue for ever making the wrong choice? Can there in such matters be a foregone conclusion? Even if God's mercy is everlasting, and never gives any man up, may there not be some men who will never yield to its influence and let themselves be brought back in repentance to God? *There may be.*

And yet, on the other hand, *there may not be.* And it seems to me that this is as far as we can go, since we only see through a glass darkly, we know in part, and our Christian faith is a working faith, which does not answer all or questions, though it gives us what we need. *For these reasons I can never rest in a dogma of everlasting punishment, nor in a dogma of conditional immortality, nor in a dogma of universal salvation, but only in the hope of the Gospel.* Heaven means the perfect beatitude of the presence of God. Hell means the outer darkness of those who shut themselves out from the presence of God by impenitence. If the one is a reality, the other is a reality. And thus 'eternal death' is a dreadful reality, in the sense that it is the ultimate tragic possibility. *But it may be that no man will ever inherit and realize it*, because it is the will of God that all men should be saved and come to the knowledge of the truth, and His infinite omnipotent love may win all men in the end. I think that is the only kind of answer that Christian faith can give to questions of final destiny.

(Unpublished Lectures on Eschatology, pp 36-42)

4 ETERNAL LIFE
by John Baillie

IT comes, then, to this – that the only knowledge we can have of eternal life is that which comes to us through our present fore-tasting of its joys. All that we know of the other life *there* is what we know of it *here*. For even here there is *another* life that may be lived, a life wholly other than that which commonly bears the name and yet one which may be lived out in this very place where I now am, be it desert or tilled field, office or market-place, study or sick-bedroom and may be begun to-day. This other life is the life everlasting ....

Of the specific conditions of its future manifestation there is nothing that we can know. Many questions may be asked but none can be answered. There is, however, one question of this kind that must not go quite unmentioned – the question whether the life everlasting is to be an *embodied* life. We have already studied the waverings of the thought of the past concerning this issue. On the one hand it has been felt that since the life we hope for is a life which will altogether transcend the present material and temporal and spatial order, material bodies like our present ones would be wholly unsuited to the conduct of it. On the other hand there has been the difficulty of conceiving how a soul can have any effective life, or can indeed exist at all, without the co-operation of its bodily organism. The Greeks were more acutely aware of the former difficulty, the Jews of the latter. But in the end the Jews were really conscious of *both* difficulties, and in that they seem to have definitely the advantage over the Greeks. Their reflection led them in the end to the position that the citizens of the Heavenly Kingdom would indeed possess bodies, but that they would be 'transfigured' bodies, 'angelic' bodies, bodies 'made of the light and glory of God'; and this was the view followed by our Lord and St Paul. If we press the question whether the body of glory is to be the same body transformed or another body which replaces it, we receive no clear of united answer. Not even St Paul, who has set out his judgment at considerable length, can be pinned down to a certain pronouncement on the point. And perhaps this is no surprise. For which of us was ever pinned down to a certain pronouncement on the parallel question at what point a stocking that has been darned and darned again ceases to be the same stocking and becomes a new one? Perhaps St Paul will not answer us because the question we put to him is too trivial for there to be any answer. Do not the bio-chemists tell us that even in the present life there is an almost complete renovation of our bodily tissues within each seven year period, so that there is no material but only a formal identity between the body I now have and the body I had seven years ago. The change to a heavenly embodiment would no doubt be of a still more radical kind – a change, as St Paul says, to something that is not flesh and blood at all: 'flesh and blood cannot inherit the Kingdom of God' (I Corinthians 15:51). And if it be true that in heaven 'they neither marry nor are given in marriage', then indeed it is difficult to believe that we are to retain to all eternity bodily organisms that have plainly been contrived for marital ends and some members of which would thus for ever remain without further function. (St Thomas Aquinas argues that when St Paul said that 'flesh and blood cannot possess the Kingdom of God', he meant only that they could not possess it until they were rendered incorruptible. Thomas therefore holds himself justified in believing that our fleshly bodies rise, and remain as fleshly, animal, and material throughout everlasting life, though being 'glorified' in certain other specified ways. The sexual members will rise with the rest of the body. 'Nor,' he goes on 'is this obviated by the fact that there will be no use for those members'; because though these members will be without use, they will not be 'without purpose, since they will serve to restore the integrity of the human body' – *Summa contra Gentiles* iv, 98; volume iv, p 300f of the translation of the English Dominican Fathers.) But on the other hand most of us will shrink no less than did St Paul from the conception of an entirely disembodied (or, as St Paul says, 'naked') spirit. The Apostle found it impossible to conceive how his spirit could live that fuller life in the hereafter to which he so eagerly looked forward, unless it were provided with some kind of bodily organization by means of which it might express itself; and the conduct of the psycho-physical debate from his day to ours has, if anything, made the entertainment of such a conception more difficult for us than it was for him. 'I know,' he writes, 'that if this earthly home of my bodily frame [*literally*, tent] be taken down, I get a building from God a home not made with hands, eternal in the heavens. And to this end I groan; I yearn for the putting-on of this heavenly structure of mine, being assured that, having put it on, I shall not be found naked' (II

Corinthians 5:1-3). St Paul's hope, then, is for a bodily endowment far more perfect in its organization, and adapted to a far higher mode of life and far more intimate mode of intercourse, than any earthly or material body could ever be; and such, it would seem, is still the most reasonable hope for us to-day (cf. Edmund Spenser's 'An Hymne in Honour of Beautie'). Yet about the nature of such a body nothing of a positive kind can ever be imagined by us. We can only say with the Apostle, 'God giveth it a body as it pleaseth Him' (I Corinthians 15:38). Our discussion may fittingly be concluded with some familiar words from the First Epistle of John: 'Beloved, now are we the sons of God, and it doth not yet appear what we shall be; but we know that, when He shall appear, we shall be like Him; for we shall see Him as He is. And every man that hath this hope in Him purifieth himself, even as He is pure' (I John 3:2-3).

(And the Life Everlasting, pp 251-255)

5 EVENING PRAYERS
by John Baillie

GRACIOUS God, I seek Thy presence at the close of another day, beseeching Thee to create a little pool of heavenly peace within my heart ere I lie down to sleep. Let all the day's excitements and anxieties now give place to a time of inward recollection, as I wait upon Thee and meditate upon Thy love.

Give me to-night, dear Father, a deeper sense of gratitude to Thee for all Thy mercies. Thy goodness to me has been wonderful. At no moment of the day have I lacked Thy gracious care. At no moment have I been called upon to stand in my own strength alone. When I was too busy with my petty concerns to remember Thee, Thou with a universe to govern wert not too busy to remember me.

I am bitterly ashamed, O God, that always I must be confessing to Thee my forgetfulness of Thee, the feebleness of my love for Thee, the fitfulness and listlessness of my desire. How many plain commandments of Thine have I this day disobeyed! How many little services of love have I withheld from Thee, O Christ, in that I withheld them from the least of these Thy brethren with whom I have had to do!

Dear Lord, if at this evening hour I think only of myself and my own condition and my own day's doings and my day's record of service, then I can find no peace before I go to sleep, but only bitterness of spirit and miserable despair. Therefore, O Father, let me think rather of Thee and rejoice that Thy love is great enough to blot out all my sins. And, O Christ, Thou Lamb of God, let me think of Thee, and lean upon Thy heavenly righteousness, taking no pleasure in what I am before Thee but only in what Thou art for me and in my stead. And, O Holy Spirit, do Thou think within me, and so move within my mind and will that as the days go by I may be more and more conformed to the righteousness of Jesus Christ my Lord; to whom be glory for ever. Amen

(*A Diary of Private Prayer*, Twenty-sixth Day)

* * *

O THOU Creator of all things that are, I lift up my heart in gratitude to Thee for this day's happiness:

For the mere joy of living:

For all the sights and sounds around me:

For the sweet peace of the country and the pleasant bustle of the town:

For friendship and good company:

For work to perform and the skill and strength to perform it:

For a time to play when the day's work was done, and for health and a glad heart to enjoy it.

Yet let me never think, O eternal Father, that I am here to stay. Let me still remember that I am a stranger and pilgrim on the earth. *For here we have no continuing city, but we seek one to come.*

Preserve me by Thy grace, good Lord, from so losing myself in the joys of earth that I may have no longing left for the purer joys of heaven. Let not the happiness of this day become a snare to my too worldly heart. And if, instead of happiness, I have to-day suffered any disappointment or defeat, if there has been any sorrow where I had hoped for joy, or sickness where I had looked for health, give me grace to accept it from Thy hand as a loving reminder that this is not my home.

I thank thee, O Lord, that Thou hast so set eternity within my heart that no earthly thing can ever satisfy me wholly. I thank Thee that every present joy is so mixed with sadness and unrest as to lead my mind upwards to the contemplation of a more perfect blessedness. And above all I thank Thee for the sure hope and promise of an endless life which Thou hast given me in the glorious gospel of Jesus Christ my Lord. Amen.

(*A Diary of Private Prayer*, Twenty-first Day)